THIS CITY IS KILLING ME

THIS CITY IS KILLING ME

Community Trauma and Toxic Stress in Urban America

Jonathan Foiles

Belt Publishing

Printed in the United States of America

First edition 2019

ISBN: 978-1-948742-47-4

Belt Publishing
3143 West 33rd Street, #6
Cleveland, Ohio 44109
www.beltpublishing.com

Book design by Meredith Pangrace
Cover by David Wilson

For ESF

"But the poor person does not exist as an inescapable fact of destiny. His or her existence is not politically neutral, and it is not ethically innocent. The poor are a byproduct of the system in which we live and for which we are responsible. They are marginalized by our social and cultural world. They are the oppressed, exploited proletariat, robbed of the fruit of their labor and despoiled of their humanity. Hence the poverty of the poor is not a call to generous relief action, but a demand that we go and build a different social order."
—Gustavo Gutiérrez

"It is a joy to be hidden and a disaster not to be found."
—Donald Winnicott

CONTENTS:

INTRODUCTION

"Do you think you can keep yourself safe?"

Jacqueline has been in my office for about ten minutes. The tears she's kept choked back begin to flow down her cheeks. She shakes her head "no" and looks down at the floor. She's been my patient for a little over a year, and in that time she's been hospitalized about once a month. This is the first time she's shown me the depths of her pain; usually her family brings her into the ER after they find a razor blade stashed under her bed or discover her with a rope around her neck.

I begin to fill out the required paperwork while thanking Jacqueline for being honest with me and praising her recovery. She asks if she can call her family. I say yes, of course, and even though I don't speak Spanish I can guess how the conversation is going. Jacqueline speaks in hushed tones. The voice on the other end sounds frazzled, almost angry. I write down in detail when she told me she wanted to kill herself, how she plans to do it, the number of times she's tried before. After a few minutes we're both ready. I put on my coat, and together we walk from the outpatient clinic where I work to the main hospital building across the street.

Jacqueline and I have been meeting weekly, and we've developed a good working relationship. It's hard for me to see her down like this, although I admire her vulnerability. According to Freud

I'm supposed to be committed to neutrality and work to contain my own wish to see Jacqueline happy again. I also remember that Freud's case notes show that he didn't practice this himself, so I decide to plunge ahead and tell her something that's been on my mind lately.

"You know, Jacqueline. I do have some news. My wife is pregnant."

She's the first patient I've told. My wife is now safely outside of the first trimester, so I no longer feel as worried by the possibility of a miscarriage. Jacqueline's face lights up instantly.

"She is? Oh my God, that's so wonderful! I know you're going to be such a great father."

The smile remains on her face as we walk into the ER, even though I've just signed an affidavit swearing that she is at imminent risk of harm. I motion her to one of the vinyl couches in the waiting room while I speak with the charge nurse, and once I am finished we sit next to one another. The television in the corner silently flashes the day's news. I show her ultrasound pictures on my cell phone while we wait for her name to be called.

The day on which I hospitalized Jacqueline was in many ways an ordinary day. I work as a therapist at a community mental health clinic on Chicago's West Side. I started out as a case manager working with adults experiencing homelessness who also had a serious mental illness. Case management gives you a crash course in the inadequacies of our social safety net, but aside from filling out paperwork and making calls I also got to learn about my clients' lives over cups of bad fast food coffee. I quickly figured out that this is what I enjoyed the most. These experiences led me to become a therapist. The clinic where I work is the outpatient psychiatric department of a safety net hospital on the West Side of Chicago. After Jacqueline was admitted, I went back across the street to the clinic and saw six other patients the same day, all with varying levels of need.

The movement to create clinics like the one where I work began in 1963 when President Kennedy signed the Community Mental Health Act. This act delegated federal funds to build community mental health centers across the country, a notable shift away from the institutional model of years prior. Kennedy's sister Rosemary underwent a forced lobotomy in 1941 that left her with the intellectual capacity of a two-year-old. I like to think that Kennedy had this in mind when he offered an alternative, humane way to treat those with mental illness.

The actual law was rather toothless and didn't lead to many notable outcomes, but it played a key symbolic role in the deinstitutionalization movement in the United States. Psychopharmacology had begun to advance beyond what was largely a guessing game into something that resembled a science. Fourteen antipsychotic medications were developed in the United States between 1954 and 1975.[1] The first two antidepressants, iproniazid and imipramine, were introduced in the 1950s.[2] These drugs were far from perfect; the earliest antipsychotics could induce irreversible Parkinsonian-like tremors and cause patients to have a need to be in constant motion (known as akathisia). Iproniazid was later found to cause liver damage and removed from the market. Nevertheless, deinstitutionalization proceeded rapidly, and while the movement should rightly be criticized for sending many patients from a bed and into homelessness, the asylums which went out of business were awful places much prone to abuse that did little to ease the suffering of those confined there.

As persons with serious mental illness were increasingly encouraged to live in their communities, the need for robust outpatient mental health services based in the community increased. Unfortunately, the growth and availability of such services did not proceed nearly as rapidly as the pace of deinstitutionalization, and the gaps in care continue to the present day. For those states with the poorest options for mental health care, providers (social workers like myself, counselors, psychiatrists, psychologists, and psychiatric nurse practitioners) would have to treat six times as many patients as those in well-funded states. Of course this is impossible, so instead people are forced to do without.

In Alabama, for instance, there is one mental health professional per 1,260 residents.[3] Alabama doesn't even rank last in terms of the percentage of the state budget allocated to mental health services; at 1.5 percent, they're ranked thirty-fifth in the nation. Arkansas is last with just 0.7 percent. Mental health services are rarely a priority and were particularly hit by cuts made in the wake of the 2008 recession; states slashed at least $4.35 billion from their mental health budgets between 2009 and 2012.[4] The most recent statistics from the Bureau of Health Workforce tracking Health Professional Shortage Areas that lack adequate healthcare estimated that 110 million Americans, roughly a third of the country (but concentrated in urban and rural areas), lack access to a psychiatrist.[5]

In this book I will focus on Chicago because it's what I know best, but there is no state, no city in America that does an adequate job taking care of its citizens with mental illness. Access to mental health services in Chicago, like so many other things, depends upon your ZIP code. If you live in one of the richest neighborhoods, such as the Gold Coast, there are 4.41 mental health professionals per 1,000 residents. Travel to the Southwest Side where I work and that figure drops to 0.17.[6] But it hasn't always been like this. In the 1960s and 1970s the city had nineteen community mental health centers spread across the city. Various mayoral administrations chipped away at this until the city was left with twelve. Then came Rahm Emanuel.

Emanuel was sworn in as mayor on May 16, 2011, and within a year he had closed six of the remaining clinics. The stated rationale was to reduce costs as part of a larger effort to trim the budget. The overall savings according to the city's own figures was estimated to be about $3 million, equaling 0.04 percent of overall expenditures that year. By that point the clinics mostly existed to serve city residents without insurance, and the majority of their patients were Black and Latinx. Emanuel and his staff promised that the 3,000 or so patients of the shuttered clinics would be able to receive services elsewhere, seemingly not accounting for the fact that mental health services in Chicago were already far from adequate. In 2016, the city privatized one of the remaining clinics, leaving Chicago with just five community mental health centers for 2.7 million people.

But Emanuel was not done. Just one year later, he closed fifty schools throughout the city, once again in primarily black and brown neighborhoods. This time, the excuse was to improve outcomes by consolidating services and eliminating poor performing schools with declining attendance. Chicago Public Schools also hoped to save money through the closings, although to date they have not shared statistics on whether or not they were successful. A 2018 study by the University of Chicago Consortium on School Research examined the primary rationale for the closings—academic test scores—and found that students from schools that were closed actually had lower test scores in their new schools, particularly in math. In addition to these quantitative statistics, the students also reported that the process felt rushed to them, left them in mourning for their communities and their schools, and created "us versus them" dynamics in their receiving schools.[7]

Alongside this reduction in access to needed social services and supports, Chicago's annual murder rate began to spike. In 2012, Emanuel's first full year in office, the total number of murders in Chicago was 436. The number hovered around 400 until 2016 when the city experienced a massive spike in violence, resulting in 771 murders. The number declined the next year, but only slightly; 650 people were murdered in 2017. Armchair experts of all stripes are quick to suggest reasons for the rapid increase, often in barely-coded racialized language, but no one has been able to identify a single trigger for the rise in violence.[8]

Closing mental health clinics, closing schools, rising rates of violence: each usually gets treated as its own story, but residents of Chicago's South and West Sides are not allowed that luxury. Chicago's murder rate did not rise in a vacuum; while it's impossible to draw causal lines from the mental health clinic or school closings to the homicide rate, it's hardly a radical thought to suggest that eliminating crucial mental health services while causing patients and schoolchildren to cross gang and community lines in order to see their therapist or simply go to school has not further endangered the lives of the city's poorest residents. We rarely talk about these issues at all, and conversations that focus upon the actual lives impacted are rarer still. This book aims to spark such a discussion.

———————

Chicago was and is a city that is deeply segregated by race. It is a common stereotype to depict the minority urban dwellers as those who are forgotten by those in power. I no longer find this depiction to be true. Rather, their lives are under constant surveillance from multiple systems and institutions. Thanks to Michelle Alexander's *The New Jim Crow*, more people are aware of the evil that is mass incarceration. The fact that 2.3 million Americans, a disproportionate number of whom are Black and Latinx, are currently imprisoned is a national shame. However, there are more than twice that number of citizens who are on parole or probation, creating a system of mass supervision that continues to control their lives long after they have supposedly paid their dues to society.[9]

The intrusion of the state on minority lives is not limited to the police or the criminal justice system, however. We often talk about "the system" or "the government" as being some singular, monolithic entity. This language only heightens its power by making it seem both inevitable and incapable of change. The system, though, has been created by people, and while we can rightly bemoan the influence of big money and corporations in our politics, the systems which we have in place today are still largely the creation of middle- and upper-class whites. Condemning the brutality of the Chicago Police Department is right and good, but if white people continue to use 911 and CPD to police the behavior of people of color we are ensuring that nothing will change.

Most are not willfully blind but rather ignorant of such things. If you live in a world where the rules are largely created by people who look like you for your benefit, it's hard to see the invisible lines setting you aside from everyone else. Many residents of Chicago will never have a negative interaction with Chicago Public Schools or interact with the Department of Child and Family Services at all (unless it's to become a foster parent), so it can be hard to know just how broken those systems are for people of color. Decades of right wing attacks against "big government" have lent a sad aura of inevitability to the failure of such bureaucracies. Perhaps they are working exactly as intended.

When one considers the history of minorities in America since its founding, one can clearly see a system that has adapted with the changing tides but always had as its goal the elevation of whites at the expense of minorities. There is nothing inevitable about this; it's the result of a number of policy decisions and ever-mutating forms of racial panic. Oppression takes many guises and sows the roots of trauma throughout generations.

You may be wondering how these broad historical trends relate to mental health on an individual basis. Our lives and our experiences shape the way we perceive the world and impact our vulnerability to depression, anxiety, and the like. We've made great strides in the ways that we've normalized experiences of mental illness, but at times these conversations obfuscate the different nature of mental disorders. If you begin vomiting one evening, you will most likely consider a number of different scenarios. Maybe you ate at a new restaurant and thought that the fish had a funny smell. Maybe the person whose desk is next to yours went home sick with the stomach flu. Eventually, though, either on your own volition or with the help of your doctor, you'll most likely be able to identify a cause rather quickly and treat the illness appropriately with rest or medication.

Diagnosing mental illness does not work like this. *The Diagnostic and Statistical Manual of Mental Disorders*, Fifth Edition (DSM-5)[10] is the book all mental health professionals use to assign a diagnosis. To merit a diagnosis of major depressive disorder, for example, you must have had at least five of the following symptoms for the preceding two weeks: persistent depressed mood, lack of pleasure in almost all activities, fluctuations in appetite, sleep disturbances, lack of energy, feelings of worthlessness, difficulty concentrating, and recurring thoughts of death. There is no one way to end up with these symptoms, though. As near as we can tell, some people are born with a genetic disposition to melancholia that can be exacerbated by life events, and others probably would not have developed clinical depression if they hadn't lost their job or gone through some other painful development. Treatment will probably not look uniform either; both psychotropic medications and therapy are effective, but depression has many permutations and what helps one person could fail to help the next.

We diagnose people, not cultures or neighborhoods, with depression. This singular focus can help obscure the environmental factors that contribute to mental illness and minimize the contributions our society makes to the mental suffering of the poor. It is far easier to feel depressed if you live in a neighborhood that has experienced chronic disinvestment, has few supportive community resources available, and is marred by gun violence.

This also makes it much more difficult to treat. How does one heal a whole neighborhood? I can do my best work as a therapist to help someone improve, but there is only so much that can be accomplished in individual therapy before we run up against the structures that continue to perpetuate such suffering. We need to cast a bigger vision.

In public health, these outside factors that impact the functioning of individuals within their communities are known as "social determinants of health." According to the Centers for Disease Control and Prevention, such factors include unstable housing, low income, unsafe neighborhoods, and poor education.[11] I will be utilizing this framework throughout the book to analyze how policy decisions and priorities have negatively influenced the mental health of my patients, but I want to take this conversation a step further.

Consider employment as an example. It's fairly obvious from the data that being unemployed or underemployed can be deleterious to one's physical and mental health.[12] One solution that is often proposed is workplace development programs. These can indeed help, but what if there simply aren't jobs located within the community because of systematic disinvestment? What if the jobs which are available are mostly within the retail and service sectors and don't pay a living wage? What if the employers refuse to hire someone who has been incarcerated? What if the jobs don't allow flexible scheduling so parents can be present for their children? And how did these communities get stuck with such poor employment options in the first place? We need a framework that recognizes these systemic issues and how they disproportionately affect people and communities of color.

We have a framework in mental health for understanding the ways in which a traumatic event can impact an individual: posttraumatic stress disorder. We haven't done nearly as good of a job at accounting for the other mechanisms by which outside events impact a person and a community's wellbeing. In this book I will talk some about individual traumas, but my focus will be upon larger traumas that occur within a community (unemployment, poverty, lack of affordable housing, violence) and within history (Jim Crow laws, mass incarceration, forced displacement, redlining).

These traumas exert a different sort of pressure upon the individual, creating what's known as toxic stress.[13] Consider this example: Two young boys are bullied at school. The first boy, "Michael," goes home with his grandmother who talks to him about it, makes him a snack, and helps him forget about it for the evening. She also resolves to address it the next day with his teacher so it doesn't become a larger issue. Michael went home in an emotionally aroused state, but due to attentive caregiving he is calm by the time he goes to sleep and isn't bothered by the time he goes to school the next morning.

"Thomas" is also bullied, but his experience is different. His caregivers have to work irregular hours to make ends meet, so when he goes home a neighbor is nearby to keep an eye on him but Thomas doesn't have anyone to talk to right away. His emotional arousal level stays high. His parents finally arrive at home, and right after dinner his father starts drinking. His stress level increases. He goes to his room because he knows what comes next. He can hear his father slapping his mother around and calling her names. He is unable to talk to anyone about being bullied, and he is more stressed when he goes to sleep than he was when he came home. He goes to school in the morning more anxious than when he left, is bullied again, and his stress skyrockets.

If these conditions continue for Thomas, he will be at great risk for both physical and mental health issues down the line. He will have a greater chance of being unemployed or underemployed, have more relational instability, express less satisfaction with his overall life, and will most likely die sooner. Now imagine communities that, because of constantly cascading waves of trauma upon every level, are made up almost entirely of Thomases. These are the conditions we have created in urban areas throughout the country.

Most therapists who work in community health look like me and not like the clients we serve. The profession is aware of this; almost every workplace as well as every licensing and accrediting body require some sort of annual training in cultural competence or, better, cultural humility. The skein of white privilege never fully reveals itself in a three-hour seminar; working at this job requires you to pay constant attention to the way in which your privileges have structured your world. My own profession, social work, has social justice as one of its core values, according to the National Association of Social Work. Still, though, the way in which we approach mental health work is often divorced from this lofty goal, if not in theory than in practice. In my own graduate program of social work, I reached a point where I had to choose between a clinical (that is, mental health-focused) or social administration (primarily policy-based) approach. The longer I work at my job, the harder it is to tell the two apart. This book is my attempt to bring both sides together.

In the pages to come, I will introduce five of my patients and demonstrate how their lives have been impacted by policies and practices outside their control. We will revisit Jacqueline, a transgender woman of color trying to survive and complete her journey to become herself. You'll also meet Frida, a deeply traumatized child who grew into a traumatized parent whose children were removed from her care by the Department of Children and Family Services; Robert, who endured trauma in the Cabrini-Green projects and refashioned a self-narrative that made him an African prince in exile; David, who failed out of a selective enrollment high school and lived amongst rats and the books he couldn't stop hoarding; and Anthony, who lost his son to a random act of gun violence and was still trying to pick up the pieces of his life years later.

I do not want you to feel sorry for my clients. I don't feel sorry for them, and I don't think they would want anyone else's sympathy either. Sympathy does nothing to change their situation in life. Rather, I want you to see them, to be forced to confront the impact that policy decisions have upon the lives of our cities' poorest residents. Their stories give me hope, yes, but even more than that they challenge me. They challenge the advantages conferred to me because of my white skin, who my parents were, where I grew up, and who I love. I chose none of those facets of my identity, and neither did they.

As is standard practice within my field, all names and identifying details have been changed. I have preserved enough of my patient's stories to illuminate my thesis but have left out or modified those details that are not relevant. Out of respect for their lives and experiences, the rest has been told exactly as it occurred.

I'm aware that by sharing these stories I risk fashioning myself into the "white savior," an outsider who comes parachuting into urban communities of color to save them from their woes. That is not my intention in writing this book, but I realize the tension inherent in the project. I will do my best within these pages to let their stories speak for themselves. I may have captured their attention for an hour every week or two as we worked together, but real lasting change can never occur in my office alone. Any progress my patients have made is due to their dedication and hard work; I am privileged to help guide them along the way and be their cheerleader. I strive to always listen to my patients without interjecting my own construct of what I think is going on, and what you will see in this book is largely a reflection of what I have learned by listening to them.

CHAPTER 1

JACQUELINE

When I first met Jacqueline, she was trying very hard to hide in our waiting room. She was wearing large Jackie Kennedy-style sunglasses, and the frayed hood of her hoodie was cinched tightly around her face despite the summer heat. She was wearing gray sweatpants, the cuffs of which were ragged and dingy from dragging on the ground behind her flip flops. Her head was tilted downward, her gaze focused tightly on a spot about six inches in front of her toes. Her mental health assessment noted that she was a transgender woman, but the intake worker did not ask her for her real name. I called out her last name like a drill sergeant and asked her to follow me back to my office.

I was excited but nervous to begin treating Jacqueline. She was the first patient I had seen with borderline personality disorder, and I had heard horror stories from other professionals about working with that population. She was also the first trans patient I treated. I had no special training in trans health or treating LGBTQ populations, but I was trans-affirming and thought I could help her. Looking back, I think I was also trying to atone for the homophobia and transphobia that had shaded my conservative Midwestern upbringing.

In my office, I try to create a safe space that comforts the patient. Plants line my shelves, and I have various art prints hanging on the wall, all in muted colors. I keep my lights low. I noticed that Jacqueline continued to keep her sunglasses on her face even though I felt certain she could barely see a thing. She had come ready to begin treatment; she had already called my supervisor several times asking to be connected with an individual therapist. She wasted no time in telling me about her traumatic past. About twenty years ago she was on vacation in her native Brazil visiting her family. At that time she was living as a gay man. She went to a local bar and had a little too much to drink. She met someone and decided to go home with him. He offered to drive her back to his place, and since she had walked to the club she accepted. Due to the lingering effects of the alcohol, the blindness of lust, or both, she didn't pay attention to where he was going. She noticed when he stopped in the middle of the field, reached behind him, and pulled out a machete. Her senses sharpened, she wrenched open the door and began running for her life. She ran through unfamiliar terrain for an hour and a half until dawn when a stranger let her use their phone.

I often ask patients when they thought their problems started. I do this not because their answer is necessarily correct, but it gives me a sense of how they think of their symptoms. Jacqueline traced the source of her mental suffering back to that day. It wasn't hard for me to see why Jacqueline felt that this marked the commencement of her downward spiral. Before then she had lived a decently fulfilling life as a gay man. She had friends, she spent most of her time in Boystown, the historically LGBTQ neighborhood in Chicago, and she was active in the dating scene. Inside she knew that she felt like a woman, and she only really felt comfortable in her own skin when she was performing her drag routine, but she didn't yet know what it was to be transgender.

As I grew to know Jacqueline better I found out that things before the attempted murder weren't quite so sunny as she remembered. She felt immense pressure during high school to act hypermasculine. This grew to be exhausting, and she finally came out as gay to her parents when she was sixteen. According to her they were shocked, but she later told me that one of the first

English words her immigrant father learned (and then deployed liberally) was "faggot," so I assume they suspected something. Regardless, they kicked her out that night. Jacqueline rarely had to sleep on the streets, but sleeping on couches and floors is still no way to live. She worked to make something of herself. She completed a year of college. Later her relationship with her parents healed somewhat, and she was invited back into their circle. She tended to gloss over all of this in session; she lived with her mother and saw her father regularly and reported all was well. I wanted to believe this for her sake, but the wounds of our past often don't heal as quickly as we would like.

Jacqueline's pain didn't end with her parents. During her twenties she was reasonably well-integrated in Chicago's LGBTQ scene, and from what she told me it sounded like she had strong friendships. Her romantic relationships were a different story. Nearly every previous boyfriend she recounted to me had abused her in some way—physically, sexually, emotionally, or all of the above. Jacqueline was vulnerable: She had little contact with her family at that time, she worked but still struggled to make ends meet, and she was Latinx in a predominantly white community. I don't know exactly how this combined to make love so difficult for her. Like many of my other patients, Jacqueline believed that she was just unlucky. Perhaps, but I find it far more likely that her vulnerability, not to mention her growing recognition that she did not belong in a man's body, made her susceptible to falling for anyone that showed interest in her. Freud believed that we have a repetition compulsion, an inner drive to keep reaching out for the flame even though we know we'll be burned. I don't believe in anything that fatalistic, but I do think the past scratches its grooves upon us, and the record keeps skipping unless we move the needle.

Jacqueline's first breakdowns began to occur around this point. Nearly every relationship ended with her either calling the police or having her now-ex-boyfriend drop her off at the emergency room doors. None of them accompanied her inside. She turned her pain inward, cutting herself to relieve the pressure that would build. Stress built upon stress, making her more vulnerable by the day. She began to see demons all around her. It was easier to believe that the world was infested by invisible evil rather than to confront the fact that it often shared a bed with her.

Jacqueline also began mental health treatment at that time. It's easy to look at her fragile state when she entered my office and conclude that her prior therapists and psychiatrists didn't do a very good job—and trust me, I've thought that too—but I don't think that's entirely fair. She achieved some level of stability in her previous clinic, and while I cringed when she told me some of the nakedly transphobic things her old therapist said to her, there were also things she really liked about her treatment there. It was close to her house, close enough that she could overcome her fear of public transportation to ride the bus a few stops to the clinic. She was also able to go there quickly if she was facing a psychiatric crisis, and often just talking to someone there for a few minutes would be enough to stabilize her. Given time, Jacqueline might have perceived the gaps in her treatment and looked for a better fit elsewhere, but she was not given that luxury. Her clinic was run by the city, and it happened to be one of the aforementioned locations quickly shuttered by Mayor Rahm Emanuel. That kicked off another spiral of hospital admissions and near-death experiences. Thankfully she survived. Many others did not.

There's a name in hospitals for patients like Jacqueline who frequently make use of emergency services: "frequent fliers." In some hospital record-keeping systems (not the one I work at, thankfully) their name is accompanied by a small airplane symbol to alert charge nurses and other emergency department staff if they haven't met the patient at a prior visit. It is helpful to know that the patient sitting before you may be reporting symptoms of suicidality, stomach pain, or the like because it is freezing outside and they need a place to stay, but this can easily tip over into disrespect and disregard for the human being sitting in front of you. All too often it becomes another way to stigmatize those with serious mental illness.

I was hoping that my work with Jacqueline would help her quickly achieve stability so she could feel safe at home again. At our third session she told me that she wanted to be admitted to the hospital but wanted to wait until her mother got off work. I wasn't entirely comfortable with this, but my supervisor gave me the go ahead. Fresh out of graduate school, I tried to engage her in a mindfulness exercise I had learned and thought would be helpful. We made it through two minutes before she begged me to stop. The demons she was hearing in her head were too loud. She had seen them leering at her in the waiting room, and they were now infiltrating her thoughts. She tried to resist them, but it became overwhelming.

Jacqueline did go to the hospital the next day. As I mentioned earlier, this became a pattern over the next year. Each time we concluded a session I checked her suicidality, but it seemed to vacillate wildly from day to day. I knew I couldn't hospitalize her forever. Instead I began to work with her to find out what she liked so much about being there.

I have been on our hospital's psychiatric floor several times to see my patients who are recovering there. It is a necessary place, of course, but also a deeply sad one. Our hospital building is very old, and to access the ward you must first walk along a narrow corridor with yellowed windows that open on the city skyline. There's a faded shuffleboard court painted upon the tiles lining the walkway, a vestige from a different era. It looks like something out of *One Flew Over the Cuckoo's Nest*. The rooms are small, airless. Each has a sink with a sheet of polished metal firmly latched to the wall to serve as a mirror, but age has dulled it to the point that you can barely make out your features. The television is on, loudly, in the common room. Someone is usually yelling. I always stop by the soda machine to treat myself before walking back to my office. It's become my ritual, and not because I need the caffeine. The place is so depressing I need something to jolt me to my senses and provide a little mental distance before I resume my regular work.

That was what I saw, but that was not how Jacqueline experienced it. For her, it was a wonderful place to be. "I wish I could just live at the hospital," she told me. She felt safe there. She enjoyed engaging with others in groups there even though she resisted attending groups in the outpatient clinic. She found the staff to be warm and affirming. She was never alone.

Jacqueline made great efforts to avoid feeling abandoned. She had a series of intense, short-lived relationships. She wasn't quite sure who she was. She had made several attempts at suicide and frequently thought about it. She had difficulties controlling her anger. She often felt empty. Many professionals had looked at that list and diagnosed Jacqueline with borderline personality disorder (BPD). In one sense, they weren't wrong; that list of the symptoms matches precisely with the *DSM-5*. BPD would be convenient in that it would capture her symptomatology, yet I never felt comfortable assigning her the diagnosis for a few key reasons.

Personality disorders are a strange beast. The *DSM-5* defines a personality disorder as "an enduring pattern of inner experience and behavior that deviates markedly from the expectations of the individual's culture, is pervasive and inflexible, has an onset in adolescence or early adulthood, is stable over time, and leads to distress or impairment." We don't think of depression as being "pervasive and inflexible"; even more serious mental illnesses like schizophrenia are fairly capable of being managed. There is no drug, no cure for a personality disorder. It simply names who you are.

A diagnosis of borderline personality disorder comes loaded with even more baggage. I have heard colleagues usually dedicated to person-first language (e.g., "person with schizophrenia" rather than "schizophrenic") refer to patients with the diagnosis as "borderlines." A recent bestselling self-help book written by a psychiatrist described dating people with BPD as "addictively exciting, and it's hard to say no to a girl who'll jump your bones in a bathroom stall, or accept a dare to flash a cop, or drink you under the table. At least until she kills your dog . . . a borderline is many things, but she is most often known as the reason men think all women are nuts."[1] A 2015 study[2] found that psychiatric nurses had less empathy for patients with borderline personality disorder than those with other mental illnesses, and psychiatrists were less likely to recommend hospitalization for suicidal ideation if a patient had borderline personality disorder. These negative attitudes actually increased the more one had professional contact with a person with BPD.

Borderline personality disorder is also a gendered diagnosis. The *DSM-5* notes that 75 percent of those diagnosed with BPD are women even though the symptoms appear to be equally present regardless of gender.[3] Childhood trauma is experienced by the majority of those diagnosed with BPD, and the more severe the trauma, the more pronounced the symptoms.[4] The symptoms of BPD seem eerily similar to the antiquated notion of hysteria, so named because it was thought that it was caused by a shifting uterus. (*Hysterika* is Greek for "uterus.") As hysteria faded into the background, BPD took its place. The diagnosis combined with the stigma often leads to women being punished for their response to abuse and assaults. It's like inventing a diagnosis of acute gunshot disorder without investigating who fired the weapon.

Jacqueline's identity as a transgender woman made the diagnosis of BPD even more punitive. It did not seem fair to Jacqueline or the rest of the transgender community to blame her for suffering the hatred and intolerance of the rest of society. As far as I could see, Jacqueline felt thrice rejected: by the culture at large for being Latinx, by her Latinx culture by being LGBTQ, and by the

LGBTQ community by being a trans woman of color.

Not feeling safe in your neighborhood can be a function of mental illness, a response to the real threat of community violence, or both. I believed Jacqueline when she said that it wasn't always safe for her to go outside dressed as a woman. According to the Human Rights Campaign, in 2017 at least 28 transgender people were murdered in the United States. (Many victims are misgendered in media and police reports, which suggests that the actual figure could be much higher.) Trans women of color are at an even greater risk of violence.[5] Two trans women were killed in Chicago in the span of six months while I was treating Jacqueline. On September 11, 2016, the body of T.T. Saffore was found near railroad tracks in West Garfield Park. Tiara Richmond (also known as Keke Collier) was shot in Englewood on February 21, 2017.[6] Jacqueline unfortunately had good reason to fear for her life every time she walked out her front door.

Chicago has several neighborhoods that are home to a significant LGBTQ population where Jacqueline might feel safer. Perhaps the most notable is Boystown, home to many of her favorite memories from the time right after she had come out.[7] Chicago's gay enclaves used to be located closer to the downtown area, but as rents increased in the late 1960s and early 1970s LGBTQ nightlife shifted north to occupy a stretch of Halsted Street. For years, Boystown was the epicenter of the annual Pride Parade and home to a variety of nonprofits that served the gay community, and in 1997 Mayor Richard M. Daley officially recognized Boystown as Chicago's gay district, installing large rainbow-colored pillars throughout the area. Boystown has steadily gentrified as societal acceptance of gay people increased, and the neighborhood is now often criticized for being very white and catering almost exclusively to gay men.

Boystown was where Jacqueline first found herself as a gay male, and she often wished to return there to live. She knew that she risked judgment as a trans woman of color, but it still felt safe to her. Years of rising rents had priced her out of the neighborhood, though, and most of the other LGBTQ-friendly neighborhoods in Chicago are similarly out of her reach. Like many of my patients with serious mental illness, Jacqueline receives federal disability payments each month, which serves as her primary source of income.

"Disability" is somewhat of a misnomer; the same name is often used to refer to two different programs. When applying for benefits as a disabled person, the applicant has to apply to two separate programs, Social Security Disability (SSDI) and Supplemental Security Income (SSI). To qualify for SSDI, you must work a certain number of years before becoming disabled and a certain amount of those years have to have occurred in the recent past. The amount you receive is variable depending upon your work history. If lack of work experience makes you ineligible for SSDI, you may qualify for SSI. As many of my patients have been experiencing mental illness for many years, the vast majority receive SSI rather than SSDI.

The maximum amount you can get for SSI is determined by the Federal Benefit Rate (FBR), which is calculated annually. For 2019, the FBR is $771 for an individual and $1,157 for a couple. Some states kick in some extra money beyond the federal limit, but the amount is usually insignificant. Keep in mind that that figure represents the *maximum* you can receive; if you receive any other form of income (which includes someone providing you with food or housing), the amount you get is deducted from the FBR. There is also a limit on resources, meaning that you cannot have more than $2,000 as an individual or $3,000 as a couple *at any time* to continue to be eligible for benefits.

When you first apply for disability, you mail in all of your materials and wait several months for someone to examine them and decide whether or not you are eligible. Most people are rejected at this stage; out of all of the patients I've treated as they went through the process, only one of them was approved on their first try. If you are denied, you have about two months to appeal. If you appeal, your case will linger for another several months until someone else takes a look at your paperwork. If they also deem you ineligible, you can appeal one more time and ask for a trial. That's assuming you make it that far; some give up and, according to a 2017 report from the *Washington Post*, 10,000 people died in fiscal year 2017 while waiting for a final decision.[8] At the end of this process, beneficiaries are only eligible for a maximum of $9,252 per year for an individual, $13,884 for a married couple. To put this in context, the latter figure is only 23 percent of the median U.S. household income ($61,372 as of September 2018). Receiving SSI can be a lifeline for many of my patients, but it also guarantees that they will continue living below the poverty line and prevents them from saving even small amounts to try to better themselves.

The average rent for a studio apartment in the cheapest neighborhood in the city (which also means one of the most dangerous neighborhoods) is $612. Even if Jacqueline could find an apartment below that rate, she would have little money left over for even the bare essentials. She would like to begin the process to officially change her gender and legal name, but that also takes money. If forced to choose between food and electricity or correcting her identification, she will, like most people, choose the former rather than the latter. Chicago House, a LGBTQ non-profit formed in the wake of the AIDS crisis, has developed a program to aid the at-risk trans population, and many of them are in the same boat as Jacqueline. Only 21 percent have been able to update all of their identification to conform to their correct name and gender identity. Transgender people experience homelessness at twice the rate of the general population. Most trans individuals experiencing homelessness at the very least experience harassment; 29 percent are turned away from homeless shelters and 22 percent are sexually assaulted there if they manage to get in.[9]

Contemporary society often pushes those who do not fit into its conventional boundaries into false selves, a concept first explored by British pediatrician Donald Winnicott in his 1960 book *The Maturational Process and the Facilitating Environment.* Inspired by Freud's *The Interpretation of Dreams*, Winnicott was the first pediatrician in the United Kingdom to complete psychoanalytic training. He became involved with the effort to evacuate children from major cities to the countryside in the midst of World War II. Winnicott was struck by how devastating the move could be on young children, and for most of the rest of his career he was interested in how the infant develops into a child and eventually an adult. He attached profound significance to the early events of one's life; even if one was no longer consciously aware of them, he believed that they continued to exert influence over the way one relates to others and forms relationships well into adulthood.

The pressure families and societies exert to ensure conformity at an early age has a similar effect on the psyche. One may be pushed to speak and write in a language that is not one's own, be pressured to regard cultural practices and traditions as 'odd' or 'un-American," be forced to sublimate essential elements of one's personality to fit in. As Winnicott notes, we all do this to some degree; the language that I use with my patients is not the language I use with my friends or my wife. I'm aware of this disparity, though, and can switch easily between personalities with opprobrium. Many others like Jacqueline don't have it so easy.

Jacqueline was the first patient who made me think about Winnicott's true and false selves. She took to describing her symptoms as the battle between "Jason"—her old masculine self who was angry, prone to self-harm, and desperately unhappy—and "Jacqueline"—her true feminine identity who was kind, happy, and loving. Right now she saw herself as in-between, an identity she called "Jackie." Her internal mood would shift between the personalities depending upon how she was feeling at any given time. Jacqueline wanted to make it clear that she did not think she actually had multiple personalities, and indeed she demonstrated no signs of dissociative identity disorder (what used to be called multiple personality disorder). Rather, she felt pressure to be a false version of herself, and it took work to resist that pressure.

One of Jacqueline's first false selves was a straight teenager. She had even gotten a past girlfriend pregnant when they were in high school, and although she did not regret the abortion that followed, she felt some regret that she had never become a parent. She then shifted into a gay male false self, slightly more comfortable but ultimately unsatisfying. It wasn't until she finally became a transgender woman that she could begin to feel like herself, but this was not nearly as easy as it may sound.

Jacqueline heard voices inside her head, and they were cruel. They told her that she was not really a woman but a man, that God hated her, that she was disgusting. On one level these are psychotic symptoms, a manifestation of her mental illness. At the same time, they were also an internalization of the pressures to maintain her false self. Her illness may have provided the form of her psychosis, but culture provided its contents.

To be clear, several communities and institutions have let Jacqueline down, but if she had had access to good, affirming, and *consistent* mental health care, things could have been very different. Instead of receiving such services, her reliance upon the social safety net often forced her to migrate from clinic to clinic. Instead of a comprehensive diagnosis that would take stock of the variety of societal pressures that helped create her suffering, she was affixed with a label that blamed it all on her. Instead of being treated humanely, she was written off as just another dramatic and manipulative borderline.

Jacqueline's discomfort with her true self meant that she found it very hard to be alone. She had lived by herself earlier in her twenties, but when her symptoms worsened she moved back in with her mother. Due to her frequent suicide attempts, she was on virtual lockdown inside her home. Her mother removed the doors from her bedroom and the bathroom. She had to ask her mother for a knife to cut her food or a razor to shave. I could sympathize with her mother's caution to a degree. Jacqueline could be quite impulsive, and I also feared what she could do with little forethought. At the same time, however, that's not much of a way to live.

I tried to address Jacqueline's inability to be alone first. Jacqueline was truly terrified of her thoughts and lived constantly saturated by stimuli to try and drown out the voices. I knew that she didn't find typical mindfulness exercises helpful, so I suggested that she find other ways to be just a little more comfortable with her interiority. Jacqueline was intensely religious but didn't attend church often (and given the homophobia and transphobia present in her tradition I thought this was probably for the best). Nevertheless, she loved to read the Bible and pray, so I reframed these activities as a way to practice mindfulness. As it was already a comfort to her, she took to this suggestion easily.

Next, I wanted to get Jacqueline out of the house. She didn't feel too safe walking around her neighborhood given the constant stream of murdered transgender women she saw in news reports. While some of this seemed like paranoia, I didn't want to put her in a situation where she could be harmed. However, I learned that she had access to a small backyard at her mother's house, so I suggested that she spend some time out there observing nature when the weather allowed. This also worked quite well for her.

When we first started working together, Jacqueline most often preferred shapeless outfits of sweatpants and t-shirts. She still had a collection of women's clothes from when she felt more confident, so I began by suggesting that she dress as herself while sitting in the backyard. This seemed to help her too, and gradually her wardrobe began to reflect how she saw herself. She enjoyed telling me about the scandalous dresses that she would wear to parties and the looks that she would get from men as she walked around the neighborhood.

Though she had previously been on hormones while living in Brazil, she had neither the time nor the energy to seek them out once she began living full-time in the United States. My background in case management had exposed me to a wide variety of the social services offered in Chicago. With Jacqueline's permission I called around to see if she could begin hormone treatment and found a non-profit in Chicago that billed public aid insurances and did not diagnose client's with "gender dysphoria" to make them eligible for their services. This non-profit, Howard Brown, provided her with good trans-affirmative care for the first time in her life.

Jacqueline has been taking her hormones for a little over a year now and feels much more feminine. The sunglasses still stay on occasionally, but not often. Her insurance will pay for gender transition surgery, but the limited number of in-network providers means that she's on a waiting list that is several years long. She's begun to put aside a portion of her meager monthly disability check in hopes that one day she will be able to pay for it herself.

Jacqueline is far from cured. She still has to be hospitalized occasionally, though more like a few times per year rather than once or twice per month. She still hears the voices and thinks about killing herself more often than I would like, but she has grown to trust me. I know that if I ask her if she is able to keep herself safe, she will answer me honestly. She doesn't fully feel like she is Jacqueline yet, but she's far closer than she used to be. Recently her mother went on a vacation for one week and left her alone in the house. It wasn't necessarily easy, but she did it. She comes to see me every week without fail. She often asks to see baby pictures. If I've gone too long without a haircut, she is sure to notice.

Chicago's annual Pride Parade is in June, and for Jacqueline it has become a family affair. She starts to plan her outfit months before, and a reminder that the Pride Parade is coming serves as a pick-me-up on dark days. Her parents and her brothers go with her, and from all I've heard they have a lovely time together. Their support still astonishes her.

Unfortunately, Jacqueline continues to be followed by the stigma of her diagnosis. She is well-known to the staff of our inpatient psychiatric unit, although she visits them far less often than before. She believes they largely see her as a person rather than a *DSM-5* label, and that has made all of the difference in her care. I have no intention of leaving my job anytime soon, and I believe the hospital will still be around for several years, but were Jacqueline to transfer her care due to a move, an insurance change, or the like, she would have to start all over. I fear that many other providers would only see her diagnosis.

At the very least, there would be other providers available for Jacqueline since she lives in a densely populated urban environment. Trans individuals who live in rural settings often fare far worse. Rural residents as a whole must contend with an overall lack of medical providers, particularly specialists like psychiatrists or therapists.[10] Even if treatment is accessible, potential patients may fear being judged or exposed through the social ties that bind together small communities, and providers who practice in such settings are less likely to be trained in how to treat LGBT populations.[11] So, of course, many do without. Rural trans individuals tend to fare the worst even amongst the LGBT community as a whole; a study in Nebraska found that the transgender population experienced higher levels of discrimination, depression, and attempted suicide compared to their gay, lesbian, and bisexual counterparts.[12] Chicago was difficult for Jacqueline in many ways, but living in such a city could also have saved her life many times over.

Jacqueline has demonstrated a remarkable ability to thrive,

but her case highlights the continuing inequities in both Chicago and the mental health system. She will have to wait several years for gender reassignment surgery because so few able surgeons take her insurance. She will most likely never be able to live in a neighborhood where she feels truly safe. She has to choose between officially changing her gender identity or taking care of the bare necessities. Chicago offers a few resources to those like Jacqueline, but the offerings are meager at best.

Despite their occasional conflicts Jacqueline benefited greatly from the support of her parents. I truly don't think she would be alive if it wasn't for their watchful care. Many of my other patients aren't so lucky.

CHAPTER 2

FRIDA

In the span of two weeks, Frida's life fell apart. Her father, who drifted between sleeping on the streets and staying in a trash-filled room in her apartment, had been found dead on the floor. A few days later, her daughter had walked out of the house without a coat in the middle of a snowstorm. Frida was gone and her boyfriend, who was supposed to be watching her two children, had fallen asleep. Police found one of her daughters wandering through the snow-choked streets and called child protective services, known in Illinois as the Department of Children and Family Services (DCFS). She and her sister were both removed from the home and placed into the care of an uncle. Feeling overwhelmed by the twin weights of her grief, Frida had swallowed a handful of her medications and then walked to her doctor's office to tell them what she did. She survived, but barely.

It took Frida six months to begin to pick up the pieces. When I first met her, she was focused and ready. Petite with a shock of purple-streaked hair, she burst into my office, talking at a rapid clip, and told me that she would do whatever it took to get her girls back. I acknowledged that this was important but encouraged her to think of ways that she would like to work on herself. She repeatedly assured me that she would attend all of her appointments and take whatever medication she had to in order to have a family again. Any homework or suggestion I gave her she did in a heartbeat.

Frankly, Frida's attitude was a bit of a shock to me at first; therapists aren't used to having patients so eager to take their advice.

In one of those initial sessions she told me that she had finally left the house to meet up with friends that week but felt guilty the entire time she was gone. She couldn't stop herself from wondering what would her kids think if they knew she was out having fun. She got drunk to try to make the feelings go away and came to her appointment hungover.

It's a good idea to never be too attached to a mental roadmap for treatment because what you as a therapist think is most important almost always changes. Over time, Frida's resolve softened somewhat. Her constantly bouncing knee told me she was becoming impatient, and I couldn't blame her. She had tried to take all of her DCFS-mandated classes at once only to be told that wasn't the point. As she relaxed, we began to establish our own rhythm and her trust of me grew.

One session she came in wearing all black with black mascara and black lipstick, a far cry from her normal rainbow-hued attire. I noted the change and asked her what had caused the sudden shift.

"I'm just feeling really mad at God now," she told me, breaking down into sobs. "My dad prayed and prayed and prayed, he went to Mass all the time, but what did that do. It didn't do shit. So I'm done with all that. I've actually been really interested in Satanism for a long time, so that's what I am now."

I was raised in the evangelical church and taught that Satan lurked around every corner, eager to spirit my soul to hell. I had since shed my belief in that pitchfork-and-horns notion of embodied evil, and while I am sure my relatives would shudder at the thought, I thought that Satanism might be healthy for her. She found in Anton LaVey–style Satanism a prioritizing of rugged individualism, which she had lacked in her upbringing. Even if I disagreed with the packaging, the lessons could stand, and it was her life and not mine anyway. I encouraged her to be honest with her feelings of anger and normalized them as part of the healing process. Over time she began to give a greater voice to these emotions as she moved forward in her journey of grief.

Anger at God is common after a death, as is anger at the deceased. Frida began to share with me her difficulties with her father. It began by being angry at him for leaving her all alone to parent her daughters, but it developed further over time. Frida, the youngest of three with two older brothers, had been molested by her oldest brother over a period of several years. I knew this from the write-up I had read of her intake interview, but I reserved discussing it in session until it seemed like Frida was ready. It turned out that her father had known about the abuse and had done little to stop it. Frida mentioned this in passing, but it joined a gradually swelling chorus of ways that her father had failed her. When he found her being intimate with one of her female friends, he beat her and told her that if she were gay she would go to hell. He was always getting into disputes with his bosses and rarely held a job for long. Frida grew up in abandoned buildings, foraging for food and clothing out of dumpsters.

At this stage in her treatment Frida took what Melanie Klein termed the *paranoid-schizoid* position in relation to her father. (I realize the terminology is terrible but please bear with me.) Klein was one of the first psychoanalysts to treat children. While most now think of infants as precious, vulnerable beings, Klein saw the earliest months of a child's life as a time of intense struggle that, if left unresolved, could lead to longstanding psychological issues. I disagree with much of the scaffolding that surrounds her work, but her idea of the paranoid-schizoid position is one I have returned to time and again. Klein believed that infants before six months of age experience profound anxiety at the world around them; everything is unfamiliar and a possible threat.[1] Their internal world is much the same; according to William Borden, "the inner world, as rendered by Klein, is a fluid, phantasmagoric landscape of gratifying and frustrating objects."[2] An infant engages in *splitting* (what we call black & white thinking or thinking in absolutes in adulthood) and sees objects as either "good" or "bad." Parents are good when they are meeting the baby's needs and bad whenever they fail to respond. The good parts are introjected, or turned inward, to form a coherent internal version of the world. The bad is located "out there" in others who represent a possible threat. This position is paranoid because of the fear of impinging harm and schizoid because it is "split" between good and bad (*schizophrenia* literally means "split brain").

Frida was initially unable to tolerate any negative idea associated with her father. Whenever she felt that their relationship was threatened somehow, she located the threat "out there": DCFS, other family members, etc. The bad parts of her father she disclaimed because they literally could not fit into her conception of him.

I began to think that Frida's father had been deeply mentally ill, and Frida seemed to suspect this, too. He moved the family around often for fear of being followed. Frida had herself been removed from the family home by DCFS as a child, but for reasons unclear to me she was returned. Her father wore several layers of clothing at a time even during the summer. He would spend long stretches of time sleeping on the streets rather than in Frida's house where he had a room, and Frida had no idea where he went. He resisted going to the doctor. After he passed the autopsy revealed that he had had stage IV lung cancer. It was unclear whether he was aware of this and had ever received proper treatment, but Frida had watched him gradually waste away until he literally dropped dead.

As we untangled her past I knew we were making real progress, but I always had the gaze of DCFS looming over my shoulder. Frida knew this too; I could watch her weigh her words carefully as we spoke. I often talked to her caseworker, Emily, who seemed nice enough. She told me that she was genuinely interested in reuniting Frida with her daughters, and I believed her. Still, the priorities of DCFS and the goals of therapy aren't always aligned. Emily wanted me to make sure that Frida realized the weight of her actions and to discuss parenting strategies and the ways she could improve her skills. We did do this to a degree, but I felt like it was also important to provide space for Frida to talk about the traumas of her own childhood. Emily didn't openly disagree with me, but I could tell that wasn't a priority for her or her agency.

Unless I have something that gravely concerns me, I prefer to let DCFS caseworkers contact me rather than reaching out myself. My role was to treat Frida, not to serve as a compliance officer for DCFS, and I believe it's important for the patient to know that I am there for them and their needs and am not evaluating their every statement to report upon their fitness as a parent. After a few weeks had passed and I had not heard from Emily, I asked Frida if anything had changed.

"Oh, she left," she told me. "She got another job somewhere else, I think. I have a new caseworker now, Donna. She told me she would call you soon."

I spoke with Donna once. Our discussion was more perfunctory than my talks with Emily, and while I had no reason to question her skills she seemed less interested in Frida than her predecessor. Time passed, and Donna left too. Subsequent caseworkers didn't reach out to me, so I got updates on Frida's case from her and wrote letters for the court appraising her progress to date. Such agency turnover is not unique; private charities contracted with DCFS such as the one that worked with Frida are responsible for 85 percent of such cases and have a 40 percent annual turnover rate.[3]

There were other outside factors that impacted Frida's case. Our work together took place against one of the worst fiscal crises ever experienced by the state of Illinois. From July 1, 2015, to August 31, 2017, Illinois did not have a complete budget. The impasse ruined the state's credit rating and crippled its social services.

DCFS remained funded due to a consent decree, albeit with significant delays in payments, but virtually every other state agency was impacted, including many that provided assistance to parents in need. Agencies were forced to slash programs and fire staff, putting added strain upon an already overburdened social safety net.

Everything seemed to slow down for Frida as the budget impasse stretched on. She was never denied services, and in that she was lucky, but she often had to wait for months before a spot opened for her in a mandated group or class. She was ordered to undergo family therapy with her children and was ready and willing to do so, but after one session her family therapist quit. She had to wait until they could fill the vacancy. I could see her resolve failing at times as she mused aloud whether or not she would ever get her children back. Outwardly I remained encouraging, while inwardly I wondered the same thing.

The Illinois budget crisis is just the latest in a nationwide series of self-imposed disasters that have lodged inequities deep into the heart of public services meant to protect at-risk children. We as a society have often agreed that children are in need of our protection but have struggled to adequately respond to that need. The first bureau charged with the protection of abused and endangered children was formed in 1875.[4] Although various laws and legal precedents had outlawed child abuse in various states, the New York Society for the Prevention of Cruelty to Children (NYSPCC) was part of a growing wave of private charity groups usually staffed by relatively well-to-do women to help the poor. These "friendly visitors" would eventually become the first social workers. When these women encountered abuse but were unsure how to respond, they contacted the American Society for the Prevention of Cruelty to Animals (ASPCA) and modeled their system upon that already-existing infrastructure for preventing animal abuse.

By 1920, around 300 private agencies modeled upon the NYSPCC had been formed across the United States, mostly concentrated in urban areas. Many of the organizations closed as donations became scarce during the Great Depression. Shortly thereafter, society as a whole began to become more open to governmental interventions in social issues during the New Deal era. It wasn't until the 1960s, however, that child abuse came to be seen as a national crisis. The federal government finally passed the Child Abuse Prevention and Treatment Act in 1974, which required every state to establish a bureau devoted to protecting children. A few years later, as concern mounted about the number of children languishing in foster care, Congress passed the Adoption Assistance and Child Welfare Act of 1980. This act prioritized keeping families intact and reuniting children with their family of origin after removal if at all possible.

Like similar agencies in other states, the priorities of the Illinois DCFS have shifted often during Frida's lifetime. When she was a child and was herself involved in DCFS, her family was kept intact despite repeated interventions. Around this time in 1990, about 24,000 children were in the care of the state. Three years later, a woman named Amanda Wallace hung her three-year-old son Joseph with an electrical cord after DCFS returned him to her home. In the year following Joseph's death, the *Chicago Tribune* ran over 100 sensationalist stories about the case. One representative example assailed "a system of judges, lawyers, social workers, and doctors that all but conspired to kill him."[5] Within fourteen months the number of children in DCFS had grown by 30 percent. The *Tribune's* work helped kick off a national conversation on the safety of children in the care of DCFS with stories appearing in ABC, CBS, NPR, *USA Today*, and *Newsweek*, among others.

By 1997, the number of children in DCFS care in Illinois had skyrocketed to 55,000. That same year, the Adoption and Safe Families Act passed at the federal level. The new law established that the goal of child welfare was no longer to almost solely focus upon reuniting children with their birth parents and pressured state child welfare agencies to move children into adoption at a quicker rate. Since the act passed, tides have shifted yet again and currently only about 16,000 children are in the custody of the state. It's unclear what has caused the decline.

Following a major child death like Joseph Wallace, DCFS and the agencies with which it contracts become extremely careful in returning children to the home. The names of the judge, case-worker, and attorney in the Wallace case all became part of the public record, and no one wants the death of a child to happen on their watch. Eventually, though, institutional memory fades, more children are returned, and then something happens to start the cycle all over again.

If DCFS feels that a home environment requires intervention but is still suitable for day-to-day living for the child, the family can be enrolled in intact family services. These services allow the family to receive counseling and case management while the child stays in the home and is closely monitored. For a time this seemed to be working well; from 2007 to 2011 only one child died while enrolled in the program. In 2012, DCFS decided to privatize the program by farming it out to various nonprofits, the agency to which Frida was assigned among them.

A seventeen-month-old girl named Semaj Crosby received the same services from a nonprofit known as Children's Home + Aid in her hometown of Joliet (located about 45 miles southwest of Chicago). In 2017, Semaj was reported missing by her mother. Her body was later found underneath a couch in her family's home where she had died from asphyxia. Later reports showed that DCFS had opened at least ten investigations at Semaj's home address, both for her and for other children who resided there. Semaj was just one of fifteen children in Illinois who died between 2012 and 2016 while their families were receiving intact family services,[6] and like Joseph Wallace's earlier death her story dominated the local news cycle. A federal consent decree is meant to prevent DCFS from assigning more than 153 new cases per year to investigators, but in the year prior to Semaj's death, two investigators in the Joliet office received 250 new cases and five others received 220.[7] Staff members were encouraged to close cases as quickly as possible. At the time of Semaj's death, the office had recently launched a contest encouraging them to compete with one another. The two staffers who closed the most cases in a month would receive a $100 gift card.[8]

It's easy to vilify DCFS caseworkers, and there is no question that some have been dangerously negligent. However, no one chooses to have a caseload of 250 new cases a year. Assuming a forty-hour workweek with no vacations (a recipe for burnout to be sure), a caseworker would have little more than 8 hours to spend on each case. And, of course, no one is given a clean slate once a new year rolls over, so they also have to make room somewhere for already-open cases as well. Case workers have to either choose to do the best they can in the little amount of time they are given or move on to a less demanding position somewhere else, further contributing to the high turnover observed in such agencies.

All of the children I have been talking about thus far are children of color. This is not an accident; one of the biggest factors predicting whether or not a child will become DCFS-involved is race. Nationwide Latinx children such as Frida's are DCFS-involved at a roughly proportional rate to their overall share of the population (24 percent),[9] but when broken down state-by-state the numbers differ widely. In Illinois, Latinx children are actually underrepresented in DCFS; Latinx children make up 25 percent of the child population of Illinois but only about 9 percent of DCFS cases.[10] This is most likely due not to social or ethnic differences but to the overall underutilization of social services by undocumented persons (who make up about 25 percent of Illinois' Latinx population).[11] When it comes to African American children, however, the story is noticeably different. Nationally, African American children make up about 14 percent of the child population but account for 23 percent of all DCFS cases. In Illinois the disparity is even starker; African American children are 15 percent of the state child population but 34 percent of all DCFS cases.

You might read all of this and think, "So what?" Yes, DCFS is overburdened, understaffed, and prone to the prejudices that plague other institutions. All of this would be worth it, though, to save the life of just one child, to have one less Joseph Wallace or Semaj Crosby. I'm a parent, so I understand this argument. I've even had it with myself a few times. It happens to overlook one crucial component, however: the efficacy of DCFS itself.

Studies on the effectiveness of DCFS have been decidedly mixed. Several researchers have found that DCFS interventions do little to help families learn how to better parent and have limited impact on the recidivism rate. A study published in 2018 found that child protective services programs were least effective when it came to addressing charges of neglect which happen to make up 75 percent of all DCFS cases (physical abuse being the reason in 17 percent of cases and sexual abuse in 8 percent).[12] Since neglect is often due to socioeconomic issues and current agency interventions do little to address such structural inequities, the system we have built doesn't work. Rather than teach parents how to parent, we have built a system that focuses on preventing egregious acts of harm but does little to help the majority of parents who are sincere in wanting the best for their children but are unsure how to get that. Most parents simply lack knowledge or means, not compassion or love. We tend to treat the end results as crimes no matter what.

It seemed clear to me that Frida's involvement in DCFS was not due to any intent to harm her child. Her home environment was chaotic which left her without any clear models of how to be a parent. At the time when most of us are focused on observing the outside world and learning how to grow and develop, she had to focus on how to survive. Frida's upbringing was virtually saturated in toxic stress, and she was still trying to figure out how to manage it all. She had what we call a skills deficit; there were facets of parenthood that she simply hadn't learned yet. Many of these crystallized together after her children were taken away to form a pattern in the eyes of the court. For instance, her daughters did not have a pediatrician. If one of them had a medical need, she would take them to the emergency room. This made much more sense when she explained her thinking; why call an already-overburdened pediatrician to have to wait for an appointment when she could have her needs addressed (fairly) immediately in the emergency department? She took pride in her willingness to spend hours in the ER at the first sign of illness from her children. She could have provided better care; she just needed someone to explain it to her.

Frida's past history of drug addiction further complicated her case. Before her children were born, she was injecting heroin daily. She claimed to have stopped cold turkey the moment she found out she was pregnant with her first child, and DCFS didn't seem to contest this. However, she had one relapse after her children were taken from her. Faced with her first weekend alone, she called an ex-boyfriend who remained an addict and spent the weekend with him. She quickly decided this was no solution, and she was the one who told DCFS about her relapse. Regardless, this now tagged her as a "substance abuser" in the system, triggering mandatory drug counseling and random urine screens.

On the matter of her parenting style, I thought that my own interests in Frida's well-being as well as those of DCFS converged, so I began to broach the topic in our sessions.

"Oh, when I'm with my girls, we just have a great time," Frida told me. "I'm not like that sort of mom who just stands by and, like, tells their kids to do this and not do that. I like to just jump in with them, and we all play together." I could picture this; Frida was rather small and, from a distance, it probably looked like three children playing together. In some sense it was. The need for childhood, for play, never goes away; in the words of Donald Winnicott, "it is play that is the universal."[13] Frida is far from my only patient who never really had a childhood, and all of them have found some way to temporarily regress in adulthood. Another patient told me about how he never had toys as a child. The moment he got his first paycheck from his high school job, he went and bought every toy that he had wanted when he was younger, hid them in his closet, and brought them out to play with them when everyone was asleep. It's fine to regress; it's why we crave physical comfort when we're experiencing pain or sadness. It's called the fetal position for a reason. The problem comes when you're not able to turn it off and on, to consciously choose to step away from adult responsibilities for only a moment or two.

Frida related to her children as a peer in ways other than playing together. I asked her once how she disciplined her children. She stridently denied ever using corporal punishment, and I had no reason to disbelieve her. Rather, she told me that when one or both of her daughters irritated her she simply ignored them. She knew she had a temper, and she knew that she never wanted her daughters to be on the receiving end of her anger. I could see the logic at work, but I could also imagine how deeply her daughters must be hurt when their mother went silent. I asked her where she learned that approach.

"From my dad," she told me. "He had a temper just like me, so I always knew when he had to walk away that he needed time to think before we could talk again."

Some of these issues had come up in Frida's play therapy with her daughters once it finally commenced. They continued to prolong her DCFS involvement. Such parenting lapses were serious, of course, but far from insurmountable. If every parent who tried to be their child's friend or struggled with disciplining them became involved with DCFS, the system would become overwhelmed and fall apart. If this were the only issue, perhaps Frida's case would have been resolved fairly quickly. There was something else, however, which the judge in her case could not seem to get over: the death of her father.

When Frida's father was found, he had fallen in his cluttered room and managed to pull debris onto his body as he fell or thrashed about for air. He had fallen in the middle of the night, but Frida had not realized that he was in the home and did not find his body until he had been dead for several hours. When she called the paramedics, they made note of the condition of his room and the length of time that he had been dead. Frida was never formally investigated or charged, but the judge continually returned to the condition in which his body was found. While the judge never stated this explicitly, we both knew what he thought: that Frida had been negligent in his care at best if not to some degree culpable in his death. To make matters worse, the judge was aware of Frida's abuse history and the fact that her father had known and done nothing about it. The inference was clear.

The judge's suspicion seemed to be insurmountable. Frida testified upon numerous occasions that she did not know her father had died, and she combed through family pictures to try to find examples of the poor state in which he kept his room. But it never sufficed. I believed Frida, though I had little to offer in such a situation. I was not treating Frida when her father was ill and dying, and merely telling the judge "I think she's telling the truth" would not accomplish much. Perhaps most importantly, I was Frida's therapist, not a lie detector or interrogator.

Life does not stop when a DCFS investigation begins. Frida no longer had her children, but she was stuck living with a boyfriend whom she believed had cost her what mattered most to her. She tried to make the relationship work for a few weeks but couldn't, so she moved out. She ran into an immediate problem, though: She didn't have a job. She had worked off-and-on, usually at temp agencies doing manual labor, but had not worked for a few years because her boyfriend was supporting her. Once that was no longer the case, she was thrust into uncertainty and instability.

She began with a suitcase and various friends' couches. She worked to scrape together the money to afford an apartment, but it could be rough going. Sometimes she would work for a few days in a row, sometimes for just a few hours. Her credit rating was pretty miserable, so many of the apartments that would theoretically be in her price range required both a security deposit and the first and last month's rent before she could sign a lease. It was several months before she could scrounge up the money to afford a place, and all the while DCFS was taking note of the fact that she was not housed. To make matters worse, Frida was also required to rent at least a two-bedroom apartment. Children obviously need space of their own, but the inequities continued to linger in my mind. If Frida was not DCFS-involved, she could have moved into a smaller apartment and saved up the money for a bigger place. Would this have been better? I don't know, but once someone has a case with DCFS so many facets of their lives come under close inspection. The system of mass supervision is largely invisible and all the more powerful for it.

Frida felt complicated about moving forward. She was worried that if her life contained anything enjoyable, if her apartment was too spacious or had a few too amenities, her daughters would think that she was happy to have them gone. She began to make every decision under the shadow of her own unhappiness. She was scared to get better because she didn't think that she deserved it.

I was happy when Frida began to open herself up to engage more socially. She began seeing someone. She said it wasn't serious, he was just someone from the neighborhood she had always had a crush on and it was fun to be with him. One session she showed up and seemed happier than usual. When I noted it, her face cracked into a smile and she told me, "I'm pregnant! And I'm going to keep it." She laid out her plans for the new baby. She hoped it would be a girl so she would have three. She had already told her daughters and they were working on names, and she had begun looking for a bigger apartment so she could be all set when the baby came. What she didn't seem to grasp was that having a baby under the shadow of DCFS complicates matters. I wish I could say that I was happy for her—and to some degree I was—but I mostly felt concerned. Frida was learning how to be a parent, albeit slowly and at DCFS's pace, and now she would have new responsibilities thrust upon her. I also began to question my own beliefs about Frida's fitness as a parent. What was once an abstract thought, something to be worked on at her own pace, now had a due date. My concern only grew when I didn't see her for the next four months.

We may be mental health professionals, but therapists can worry with the best of them. I feared for Frida, and since by this point I had lost all contact with her DCFS caseworker I wasn't receiving updates from that end either. Eventually she faded from view, I'm sorry to say. The need in our community is so high that I have little time to save a space for someone; there is always the waiting list or an intake waiting to begin individual therapy. Frida got to me, though, and my thoughts still wandered to her and her daughters upon occasion. The front desk handles my schedule, so when I turned on my computer one morning to find an afternoon appointment with her on my schedule I felt relieved. When she showed up I noticed her flat stomach and her depressed mood, but I wanted her to tell me on her own terms rather than pry.

I let her settle into the silence of my office. Once she sat down, she rattled off in a matter-of-fact way, "So, I lost the baby. I had a miscarriage. And then I just felt so down, like I had just lost my family again, that I relapsed. My boyfriend, see, he has some connections, and so he was able to get me some heroin. To be honest, I don't really remember much about the past two months, it was all just kind of a blur."

I cared about the personal impact of Frida's relapse. I couldn't help but think it would add further substance abuse classes to her DCFS requirements, extending the time she would be without her children. The judge in her case continued to perseverate over the death of her father, and I could tell that Frida was getting tired of it. In some way I thought that the amount of sober time she had made was noteworthy in itself, but of course I could not convince the court of that. The law rarely is able to discern the shades of gray that make up the vast majority of our lives. We mourned together, both for the baby she had lost and the continuing time away from her children.

Navigating the ins and outs of DCFS was not something I was taught in grad school, so I leaned heavily on my supervisor for help. I'd often discuss the progress we were making and complain about the accompanying lack of progress on the state's side in my weekly supervisory sessions. I was in one such session shortly after Frida returned to treatment when my supervisor said rather matter-of-factly, "You know she's not going to get her kids back, right? You need to work to prepare her for it."

I knew. I didn't know that I knew until she mentioned it, but as I thought about what she said I realized that I could see no end in sight. I introduced the possibility that Frida would lose parental rights gently, framing it as a wise way to prepare for the worst-case scenario to increase her resiliency. Of course I never told her my suspicion; such speculation would be deeply inappropriate no matter how well-founded. Even without hearing me say it, Frida seemed to be coming to the same realization. The fighting spirit with which she had strode into my office nearly two years earlier was gone. She looked tired, haggard. I wasn't surprised when she came into my office one day a few weeks later and told me that she had decided to sign over her parental rights to her uncle. She would still be able to be involved with her children, she reasoned, and they would no longer have to deal with the stress of their lives being interrupted. It was one of the hardest and most adult decisions a parent can make.

Frida missed our next session. And then she missed the one after that, and another one. She was gone for several months before I saw her again. She had experienced another relapse, she told me. She was now living in a homeless shelter for women who were dealing with substance abuse. She was also seven months pregnant. I hope she's doing well. She didn't show up for her next appointment, nor did she answer my calls or my emails. I haven't seen her since.

———————————

The Chicago Tribune recently published another piece on DCFS. A white mother in suburban Wilmette had a DCFS call made against her because someone saw her eight-year-old daughter walking the family dog alone. The article ominously notes that "mothers in the Chicago area and across the country have found themselves at the center of investigations by police or child welfare officials after their children were spotted alone but unharmed—playing in parks or left for minutes in a car parked outside a store—activities that could pass for typical or harmless but now are perceived by some as unacceptable."[14] Most of us can agree that the person who made the call was rather ridiculous. It is unmistakably disturbing to be the subject of a DCFS investigation, but in this case the system worked exactly as it should: The call was investigated, the allegations were deemed unfounded, and the case was closed.

A number of my patients have also been subjected to frivolous DCFS investigations. It is a source of stress for the parent and can trigger much worse outcomes for the children, as in Frida's case, but the solution is not as obvious as is might seem. Were we to increase the threshold for DCFS involvement, and then one day—perhaps not soon but eventually—a child will die because of the eased restrictions. The same cycle will then start all over again, and it's not the suburban mothers of the world that will be caught up in it but the Fridas.

Children are deeply vulnerable, and it's right that we as a society have taken steps to safeguard them. But we haven't done enough. Frida experienced a deeply traumatic childhood where help seemed curiously absent. She grew into an adult who was deeply traumatized, who sometimes regressed into childhood to protect herself from being hurt. She loved her children fiercely, but she needed help in knowing how to raise them. Ideally this could be part of the mandate for DCFS, but a chronic lack of resources combined with a focus on preventing abuse rather than building hard skills makes them ill-suited to help. Nothing less than a drastic restructuring of the ways that we intervene in intact families and the services we offer will prevent further outcomes like Frida, both for the parents who are trying to make it and the abused children who grow up and become parents.

I wasn't a parent when I was treating Frida, but I've since become one. I still remember the feeling when the hospital let our daughter sleep (or, perhaps more accurately, "sleep") in our room the night she was born. My wife and I were amazed that this living being, *sans* any monitors or wires or other such equipment to make sure she was alive and breathing, was entrusted to our care. I grew up in a mostly intact family and have a positive relationship with both of my parents and that still couldn't prepare me for what it's like to be responsible for another life. Parents like Frida are at a permanent disadvantage through no fault of their own, and the systems that we have in place do little to help them develop the skills they could almost certainly learn.

My wife and I are friends with some foster parents. One couple have been fostering two girls for the past few years. Recently they announced on social media that the adoption process had finally gone through, and they celebrated by showing their faces in a picture of their new family. (Foster parents are not allowed to post identifying pictures of their foster children on social media.) I knew of their love for the girls and of the struggles and paperwork required to bring them into their family. I was (and am) glad for them, but as I looked at the picture it sank in that somewhere else in the city, another Frida had just lost custody of her daughters. Maybe it was for good reason, but maybe not. Regardless of her particular situation, I still wonder about what she went through and the pain she must be experiencing every time I see the smiling faces of her children on my Facebook feed.

CHAPTER 3

ROBERT

When I started out at my clinic as an intern, my supervisor gave me a list of four clients that would become my first individual therapy cases, mostly young men with depression or anxiety. Only one of them responded to my phone calls, so my supervisor gave me the go-ahead to look through the waitlist and choose more potential patients. At that time our waitlist was extensive and not well organized. Most of my first few weeks were spent reading through mental health assessments. I knew that I wanted to take on challenging clients so that I could learn how to work with them while receiving more supervision than I would likely get at any other point in my career. That was how I first encountered Robert.

Mental health assessments are usually dry affairs; they're medical records, after all. Robert's, on the other hand, read like a novel. He was coming to our clinic to treat posttraumatic stress disorder. He had told the intake worker that he was born to an African prince via in vitro fertilization roughly fifty years ago but was kidnapped from the hospital while a newborn by African Americans who were seeking to overthrow his royal father's reign. These individuals had tortured him throughout his childhood as a means of enacting revenge upon his family. They also stood in the way of him inheriting the vast wealth to which he was entitled. As an adult, he had four sons birthed by four different women at the exact same time and had married the actress Sophie Okonedo in a secret ceremony before she became well-known. He believed they were still married.

I was not unaccustomed to working with people like Robert. Most of the homeless clients I had worked with in my first internship were suffering deeply, and some had delusions like Robert. They could be difficult, yes, but helping people was why I had entered this field in the first place. I brought Robert's case to my supervisor and asked for her approval to reach out to him. At first she was somewhat incredulous: "You really think you can handle this?" When I assured her that I could, she gave me the go-ahead.

I didn't know what Robert looked like, but when I stepped into the waiting room to call his name I had a pretty good idea which patient he was. He was a small man with eager eyes and a wide smile. He wore a brightly colored dashiki with a neatly paired kufi cap. He jumped up from his seat and followed me back to my office. When we started talking, he seemed to be affecting a baritone and spoke in a sing-song cadence.

I thought Robert might hesitate to induct me into his narrative, but he burst forth almost immediately with his life story. More than anything he wanted a witness to his experiences and to his pain. His tale was remarkably consistent with what he had told the intake worker a few months ago. Alongside sharing his past, he wanted me to know more about the current source of his troubles: African Americans.

According to Robert, African Americans were lazy. They stank. They sought to pull down those they deemed overachievers. They were vulgar. And crucially, they weren't truly African due to miscegenation during the era of chattel slavery. A verbatim transcript of our conversation would resemble a talk with Richard Spencer or David Duke. Thus, I began our sessions from a place of curiosity, wondering what had so damaged him so that he would cut himself off from his own race and what psychic toll such a split might cause.

Robert was often willing to discuss the very real trauma-related symptoms he experienced and to find some coping solutions.

Whether the source of one's pain is real, imagined, or obscured by a false narrative has little to do with how it can impact one's life or the tools that might help. Robert was happy to work on this if he had had a normal day, but if any perceived conflict or slight with an African American occurred that day or en route to his appointment it would dominate the vast majority of our time together. Since Robert lived in a predominantly African American neighborhood and traveled for an hour via public transportation for our appointments, the odds were quite good that he would have some experience he wished to discuss first. During those sessions I could hardly insert a word, Robert barely pausing for breath between invectives.

I reported back weekly to my supervisor on our work together and how I felt about working with him. After I had been seeing him for a few months with still little sense of how his self-narrative cohered, she suggested that I ask him to write a biographical statement. Robert loved the idea, and he spent several weeks working on it, updating me at each session upon his progress.

After about a month had elapsed, he presented me with a stack of Post-It notes. There was some order to them, but not much. This was how Robert saw his story, as a series of fleeting fragments that he could not unify. That was what had brought him to my office in the first place. As I read through them, for the first time I began to wonder if I was up to the task.

Robert reported that as a child he was deprived of food, water, and fresh air, made to wear dead rats strapped to his body so he would smell and grow to hate himself. He claimed that his real birthday was December 25 rather than the false birthday of February 14 (the date in his medical records) that his captors had given to him. He described horrific episodes of physical, emotional, and sexual abuse alongside more incredulous episodes such as being next to his biological father during an assassination attempt. His writing remained vivid throughout; he matter-of-factly described what it felt like to be covered by brain matter after his father's bodyguards murdered his would-be assassins and how he had witnessed the beheading of the member of the royal court who had arranged his father's attempted murder. Alongside the recurring theme of his royal roots, another note sounded throughout his tale of his captivity:

> "I was abducted when the woman took me to the hospital next to her house at Cabrini-Green and told them that I had been born at home in the bathtub."

> "A Caucasian woman came to our apartment in Cabrini-Green and swabbed my cheek for a DNA sample."

> "They took me to the broken-down elevator on our floor in the tower and raped me."

Cabrini-Green is a public housing complex on Chicago's Near North Side. For most of my childhood, it was the emblem of all that was scary and threatening about Chicago.[1] On July 17, 1970, two police officers patrolling the towers were gunned down in a field by a sniper lurking in one of the top floors. In an article about their murders, the *Chicago Tribune* described Cabrini-Green as "a Hydra's head of problems and, like the mythical monster, as one problem is cut away, two more come to take its place." In 1986, the paper referred to the housing project as "one of the country's most spectacular examples of failed public housing."

Cabrini-Green was infamous not just nationally but internationally. When the British director Bernard Rose was seeking to adapt Clive Barker's horror story "Candyman," he transposed the setting from Barker's Liverpool to Cabrini-Green. When asked why in a 2015 interview, Rose responded that he chose Cabrini-Green because it was "an incredible arena for a horror movie because it was a place of such palpable fear."[2] But Cabrini-Green was also home for thousands of Chicago residents. Any story of its decline must also account for how it ended up that way.

Before Cabrini-Green was built, the area was home to a predominantly Italian slum nicknamed "Little Hell." The push to tear down the slums and build housing towers in their place was led not by bureaucrats and politicians but by the then–politically left Chicago Housing Authority (CHA), staffed mostly by well-meaning social workers. Construction on the projects coincided with the end of World War II, and veterans were given first priority upon completion. The nearby factories that had employed the residents of Little Hell were still active, so Cabrini-Green was largely filled with working families when the towers were opened. The CHA tried to maintain the neighborhood population balance of 80 percent white and 20 percent black inhabitants and otherwise allowed residents to mingle freely. White residents despised this so-called "social experiment," however, and sought with some success to segregate blacks in their own towers.

The racial tension present in Cabrini-Green reflected the animus that played far too large a role in city politics. Aldermen resisted any efforts to build public housing in majority-white neighborhoods. The CHA, which was overwhelmingly white, at first resisted but eventually acquiesced. Beginning in 1950, no new public housing was erected in majority white neighborhoods; all new developments were restricted to the South and West Sides. This practice would eventually be challenged in the 1966 lawsuit *Gautreaux v. Chicago Housing Authority*, where the Chicago Housing Authority was found to be violating the law. Mayor Richard J. Daley responded by virtually ending construction of new public housing developments.

White flight combined with a gradual decline of manufacturing jobs across the city completed the transition of Cabrini-Green to an almost entirely black development. The median income per resident had dropped from 64 percent of the citywide average in 1950 to 37 percent by 1970. As the city's rent receipts declined, they took steps to reduce their overhead. The beautifully landscaped land around the towers was paved over with blacktop. Major and minor repairs were slow in coming, if they happened at all. The elevators almost never worked. As a safety measure, the balconies of each tower were fenced in from top to bottom with chicken wire, giving them the appearance of prisons or animal cages.

As residents moved into Cabrini-Green from across the South and West Sides, rival gangs suddenly found themselves living next to one another and began to fight for control of the housing project. Tensions between Cabrini-Green residents and the police grew increasingly worse, and high-profile murders such as the aforementioned 1970 incident only further solidified Cabrini-Green's reputation as a place of violent lawlessness.

But that's only part of the story. Thousands of residents called Cabrini-Green home, and despite its violence and the often-deplorable condition in which the CHA maintained the apartments, it remained home for them. Anyone who has a conflicted relationship with their hometown can surely relate. Dolores Wilson, one of the first Black residents of Cabrini-Green, remembers the drum and bugle corps her husband started, the building council she led to improve conditions in her building, and the murder of her son in front of their church. None of that made her think of leaving:

"Not too long after my son got killed, must have been in the fall of '91, I was at a benefit dinner, something to do with my community work, and this reporter came up to me and said, 'Aren't you Ms. Wilson?' When I said that I was, he said, 'Aren't you afraid of living in Cabrini with all this shooting and stuff?' I said, 'No. I even leave out at night and go to the store...Only time I'm afraid is when I'm outside of the community...If I'm going to live somewhere all these years and be scared, I'm crazy."[3]

Residents like Ms. Wilson were not blind to Cabrini-Green's problems, but they were committed to staying and trying to fix them. The question was whether or not the city would allow that to happen.

Because Cabrini-Green was one of the few public housing developments outside of a majority-black neighborhood, the land upon which it was located became increasingly valuable. Just a few blocks to the east lay one of the richest neighborhoods in the city, the aptly named Gold Coast. Cabrini-Green's proximity to money greatly magnified the push to demolish the projects every time a violent episode made its way into the news. Residents such as Dolores Wilson spent much of the 1990s resisting calls for demolition, but Cabrini-Green's fate was sealed in 2000 when Mayor Richard M. Daley announced the CHA's Plan for Transformation. Daley's plan called for transitioning Cabrini-Green and most other housing projects to mixed-income residences, where some would pay a rate based upon their income and others would pay the current market rate. The Department of Housing and Urban Development gave the city $1.5 billion to rehabilitate or replace 25,000 units of public housing within ten years.

As of 2017, only 7.81 percent of the households impacted by the Plan for Transformation live in those mixed-income developments.[4] Of the remaining former residents, over a third are living without a government subsidy at all. While some may have increased their income to the point where they could afford a decent market-rate apartment, it's likely that most now live in privately owned apartments where the conditions are worse. Others have become homeless. Continued demand for public housing supports this. When the CHA briefly opened up their waitlist in

2014, 280,000 people registered. Roughly 10 percent of the city's entire population got in line for the glimmer of hope provided by having their name on a list somewhere with no guarantee of actual results.

Despite the overwhelming need for housing, the CHA has let many vacant units stay empty; as of 2015, 16 percent of the available units, about 3,500 altogether, were unavailable. Due to the way in which public housing is funded, the CHA receives federal dollars per unit regardless of whether or not they are inhabited. Meanwhile, the CHA is flush with cash; they have paid off almost all of their debt and contributed far more than was required into the city's pension system.[5] Construction on new units was already slow under Richard M. Daley, but it almost stopped under Rahm Emanuel. Instead, the city is moving forward with plans to build tiny houses on vacant lots to house those experiencing homelessness after they were roundly criticized for destroying tent encampments across the city and fencing off the areas to keep them uninhabited.[6]

―――――――

Finding out that Robert had grown up in Cabrini-Green didn't necessarily mean anything. Thousands of people, including several of my other patients, grew up there or in one of the other Chicago Housing Authority high-rises, and their experiences aren't homogeneous. Most of them, however, experienced some sort of trauma associated with living there. To live in Cabrini-Green or any of the other housing projects was to be constantly reminded that you didn't matter; you had only to look at the elevators that didn't work, the graffiti and trash that congregated in the hallways, the crime that grew because the police essentially abandoned the towers and let them fend for themselves. When the police did try to intervene, it more often took the form of surprise knockdown raids rather than the daily work of community policing, hardly restoring trust in their ability to protect and serve.

I could see how a quiet, reserved, quirky child like a young Robert could be ignored. I could imagine how DCFS could fail to intervene, letting him slip through the cracks. I couldn't imagine the horrors he must have witnessed and the trauma inflicted upon his body, but I believed him. And I could see how, given all of that, he could grow up thinking that he had to be special, different, to be the target of his caregivers' ire. How he must have hoped he had a special father far away who loved him and would give anything to rescue him from his terror.

According to the French psychoanalyst Jacques Lacan, trauma is that which resists words[7]; it is, in the words of the Lacanian therapist Annie Rogers, "the unsayable."[8] Our body manages to find ways to speak even if our tongue cannot, and I came to see Robert's delusional system as a series of metaphors for his experience. Seeing how his caregivers (I assume his parents, but one can never be sure) mistreated him and the other children, they must have seemed like cannibals dining upon the children's flesh, one of the more graphic scenes he recounted for me. His birth father singlehandedly saving him from his would-be assassins was akin to imagining Superman as his father, always ready to swoop in to protect him from harm. The ways in which he felt out of place became vivid reminders that he was not from here, he was different, special. And the hatred he felt for African Americans reflected how deeply the trauma he had experienced had split his consciousness to the point where he disavowed his race to separate himself from his past as much as possible.

All of this is a construct, of course. Therapy involves making a story from a patient's experience, hazarding a theory about how things got to be the way they are and what we can do to provide healing. I do this for all of my patients, usually mentally but sometimes working it out with a group or writing it down. I don't mind sharing it with them; I have a policy of answering most questions they may ask as long as we can discuss it afterwards. Typically, though, they don't care, and I think that were I to talk of Lacan or Winnicott with most of my patients their eyes would glaze over.

When I've discussed Robert's case with fellow clinicians, they invariably have the same question: "Did he ask you if you believed him?" Over the course of the three or so years we worked together he didn't, at least not directly. Robert did share with me how involved he was in the life of his daughter, and while I couldn't be sure I thought she was probably his only child. Based upon what Robert told me, my assumption was that she had grown up with her mother, only occasionally seeing her father, and had decided to establish greater contact once she became an adult. She didn't believe Robert's story, he told me, and it seemed that she responded to him with some concern and apprehension.

On one level I believe this was a straightforward statement of fact, but I also think it was Robert's way of testing my own reaction. According to Freud, patients come to treat their therapists like the other people in their lives, which provides a key for understanding the relationships they would like to heal and for analyzing their own behavior within those relationships. Freud called this process *transference*, and I believed it was what I was witnessing with Robert. I asked him if he could tolerate his daughter never believing him. It would hurt him somewhat, he admitted, but he could; it was worth it just to have her in his life again. Over time I think his daughter's position softened somewhat, not out of persuasion but out of love. We never confronted the question of whether or not I believed him, but holding a space every week for him to talk and be heard without judgment or a prior agenda was enough for him.

My own internal push to discover the truth of Robert's life also began to disappear. It's a rule of thumb in therapy circles that you should never directly challenge someone's delusional system because it's almost always countertherapeutic. If I sincerely believe that the government is monitoring all of my communications and inserting ideas into my head, am I more likely to believe someone I barely know who tells me that that is not true or to assume that they are also a part of the conspiracy? In my experience people who experience delusions aren't usually looking for someone to confirm them anyway. Being able to treat Robert successfully and make him feel more comfortable with his own life didn't require me to excavate the outline of his biography from what he gave me. If I had a question that could impact our work together I felt free to ask, but I imposed a mental filter upon myself to weed out any self-serving curiosity.

For these reasons I largely chose not to challenge Robert on the complex of beliefs that guided his life. Rather, I focused on helping him to live better within the world he had created. This also meant coming to terms with the fact that I would never know a large swath of Robert's life and experiences. Before he had come to live in his current subsidized apartment, he had been homeless for an extended period. At some point during these years, he had also gotten an associate's degree from a city college. I couldn't find a way to harmonize these bits of knowledge that he offered me, but I worked on giving up my own need to know.

For the entirety of the time we worked together, Robert lived in a housing complex for people transitioning out of homelessness. If the program he was a part of was anything like other such programs I knew, he had probably waited years for his apartment. It showed in the pride he took in having a place of his own, sharing with me how he had decorated it and the choices he had made to make it a hospitable environment for his daughter. He could never outrun his delusional system, though, and he feared that relatives of his kidnappers were living in the building and seeking to do him harm.

Did one of Robert's relatives, one of his abusers, live with him? Possibly, although this seemed unlikely. Rather than try to get to the bottom of what was really going on, though, I focused my efforts on helping Robert to live better within his role. This man whom he feared seeing was gone from the building during the day, so we worked out a schedule for Robert that would allow him to avoid the man in the hallway. The building had optional monthly meetings for residents, and Robert decided not to go. He had a case manager whom he liked who told him any information that he missed. When Robert did happen to encounter this other individual, he chose not to talk to him but to slip by quietly and ignore any efforts he made to engage Robert in conversation. And it seemed to work; Robert reported less conflict with his neighbors, and his trauma-related symptoms began to decrease. His neighbors probably thought he was rather odd, but the tradeoff seemed more than worth it.

Robert and I also developed coping strategies for his nightmares and flashbacks. Even if the content was fictional, the terror he experienced was not. I taught Robert some simple meditation exercises that he embraced quickly. Having a preexisting interest in natural medicine and other related pursuits, he began to buy essential oils to perfume his house and soothe himself. I remain skeptical of the supposed therapeutic benefit of such things, but the placebo effect works wonders for the efficacy of many "legitimate" drugs, and I could tell that Robert was really improving. Our sessions became guided less by what Robert had endured in the past and more about what he envisioned for his future.

Our work together drew to a close not because of the progress Robert had made, although he had, but due to insurance issues. Shortly after the Affordable Care Act passed and Illinois participated in the Medicaid expansion program, the number of insurances available to my patients exploded. I have a two-sided spreadsheet pinned next to my computer showing every insurance my clinic takes and the services for which they will reimburse us. Not all insurances are created equal. Some never paid us for services, so we stopped taking them. Others fell behind on payments, causing my patients to receive bills in the mail for thousands of dollars of services (though no patient ever had to pay such charges in the end).

Robert got swept up in the mess of Medicaid expansion and was guided to one of the few insurances we do not take. But Robert and I had discussed termination before the change took effect. He had begun to miss appointments more frequently, and I suspected that he was self-terminating. He had received what he needed for me, and our time together no longer seemed as vital to his schedule. I considered it a sign of progress.

One of the last times I saw Robert he shared with me how his weekend went. He had walked to a nearby park, one of several that dot the Lake Michigan shore. It was a beautiful cloudless day, and the temperature was perfect. He sat on a park bench and took it all in. Nothing remarkable happened, but he became present to the rhythms of everyday life in a way that few of us manage to attend to on a regular basis. As he recounted this to me, I was reminded of Emerson's eyeball: "Standing on the bare ground,—my head bathed by the blithe air, and uplifted into infinite spaces,—all mean egotism vanishes. I become a transparent eyeball; I am nothing; I see all; the currents of the Universal Being circulate through me; I am part or parcel of God."[9]

I saw Robert transform from a scared, lonely man to someone on the pathway to healing and a life he had always wanted. I'll never know what exactly caused him to experience the symptoms that brought him to my office. I think of his story as a Cabrini-Green story, but probably not just for the obvious reason. He most likely endured unspeakable trauma there, but he also endured and found hope. Both were birthed in those long-gone towers.

I recently visited the site where Cabrini-Green was located.

It's now a Target. As I walked through the store's aisles, I thought of all of the lives that had passed beneath my feet. How many Roberts were created by the decades of Chicago Housing Authority mismanagement and the outright hostility the rest of the city displayed towards residents of the projects? It says something about the soul of a city that our leaders are willing to literally rob people of their homes to replace them with bright, shiny businesses. The Target is nice, but it is no home. The towers were torn down in the name of progress, but that progress has yet to arrive for most of the people who lived there.

CHAPTER 4

LUIS

The relationship between patient and therapist is unlike many others. Rather than approaching one another on equal footing, patients give me access to the scope of their lives while usually knowing little about my own. When a client has been at our clinic for several years and is transferred to my care, I am able to access their records and see what sort of progress they have made thus far. This used to feel obtrusive to me, but I've come to find that clients usually appreciate it because it doesn't feel like starting over from the very beginning. It's also necessary given the reality of the community mental health profession: therapists don't tend to stay in their jobs very long.

When I was preparing to begin Luis' treatment, I wasn't his second, third, or even fourth therapist here, but rather his fifth. In the eight years he had been in treatment so far, he had begun with a student intern who left after one year, been transferred to another clinician with whom he worked for several years, transferred to someone else after she left, and then finally made his way to me after the most recent clinician was terminated due to an (unrelated) ethical lapse. Luis was assigned to my caseload by my supervisor, and as I was perusing past therapy notes a sentence leapt out at me: "Client says that he could not imagine seeing a male therapist as it would feel like 'kissing a guy.'"

Therapists want to respect the client's wishes for their treatment, at least to a degree. If a client has been sexually assaulted by a male, working with a male therapist may inhibit their recovery. Older adults sometimes (but not always) prefer to work with someone mid-career rather than a therapist who is just starting out. Luis's stated preference was not due to age or past experience. Rather, he was prone to erotic delusions, and his lack of interest in working with a male therapist seemed to stem from his habit of being sexually attracted to his prior providers. My supervisor has worked at our clinic for several years and was familiar with Luis and his needs from a distance, and she thought that I would be the best fit among the available therapists. We agreed to start Luis out with me and see how it went.

Luis arrived to our first appointment fifteen minutes late, a pattern that would continue to repeat itself throughout his treatment. It was summer and he was drenched in sweat from the two-mile walk he had just made to our clinic. It looked like he hadn't showered for a few weeks, and I would later find out that this was indeed the case. His shoes had nickel-sized holes in both soles. He was affable if a bit distant, nothing I hadn't expected. As we walked into my office, he pointed at one of the prints I have hanging on my wall and asked, "Picasso, right?" It was, and he was the first person to notice.

I felt reasonably confident of my credentials by this point in my career, but Luis wasn't convinced. "No offense, but are you sure you can help me? You look young," he said almost immediately after sitting down. I explained to him my experience thus far, both my education and the amount of time I had been in my current role. He wasn't entirely reassured, I could tell, but it did seem to settle him somewhat. Since we had already landed on the topic, I brought up the difficulties he thought he might face with a male therapist. He looked a little shocked that his prior therapist had saw fit to include it in his notes, but he smiled and said, "Well, yeah, of course." It did not seem as self-evident to me as it did to him, but he said that he was willing to work with me.

Luis wanted to begin by addressing his hoarding behaviors. I figured I would start from the obvious point and ask him what he hoarded and why. He had a collection of neighborhood newspapers, flyers announcing local events, books upon books that he had never read. When I asked what drew him to collect those things above others, he answered, "Because it's history, it's the story of our neighborhood, of Chicago. Just think how many articles and local newspapers get published and then just thrown away." Tearing up, he told me, "I want to create a database of all of them, scan them in or something, so it doesn't all disappear. I hate to see knowledge go to waste."

Luis' hoarding had come to define him. He told me that his apartment was infested with vermin. Rats crawled through his papers at night. As soon as he turned his lights off to sleep he could hear them rustling throughout his room, and he would find their excrement upon waking. He slept next to a cardboard box of decaying books that was teeming with bedbugs and cockroaches. I began to suggest various ways to deal with the problem when he interjected, "It really doesn't bother me. I mean, I don't like to get bitten, but it's fine." He described the rats in even warmer terms, as friends of sorts. He admired their tenacity, had come to think of them as pets. He felt worried about what would happen to them if he cleaned up.

Luis' comments instantly brought to mind one of Freud's case studies of a patient who came to be called the Rat Man. Freud wrote an article[1] describing a six-month analysis of a patient named Ernst Lanzer who obsessed over a fear of his father dying (though his father had in fact been dead for many years) or something terrible happening to the woman he loved. Lanzer's obsessions were triggered by a particular story he had once heard from an army officer about a form of punishment in which a pot containing rats was turned upside down upon the buttocks of a criminal. The rat would then seek to escape by tunneling through the victim's anus. Freud believed rats had accumulated a tangled system of meanings for Lanzer, which he helped unlock through free association. I saw resonances of this case in my own work with Luis.

I don't typically assign "homework" to my clients, not really out of any theoretical allegiance but simply because my previous therapists never did for me and I try to not ask my clients to do things I wouldn't want to do. Luis's previous therapists had, though, and he asked me to set mutual goals at the end of each session. Figuring that this was something he had found helpful in the past, I readily assented to it and together we identified how much trash he would dispose between our sessions.

Two weeks later, he came back and reported that he hadn't been able to do it. I thanked him for his honesty, and we renewed our goals for the next session. Again he didn't do them, and this set a pattern in his treatment. After several sessions, I suggested that we revisit the goals and try to make them more attainable. It seemed obvious to me that we had been aiming too high, and I worried that Luis would grow discouraged at the lack of progress. Appearing somewhat incensed by my suggestion, he stated that he did not want to change them at all and he would do it by next week. Of course, he did not.

Hoarding took up the bulk of our earlier work, but it wasn't the only thing Luis wanted to talk about. He was frequently grandiose and loved to tell me of all that he planned to accomplish in the very near future. I had also seen there was a note in his file stating that his preferred name wasn't Luis but Samuel and asked what he would prefer I call him. "Luis is fine for now, I just hate the fact that I'm named after my father so I've thought about changing it. He's a real asshole." This sounded like something worth addressing, so over the course of several sessions we explored his relationship with his father.

Luis' father was abusive, physically and emotionally, and his mother refused to intervene. I suspected that she may have been scared of Luis's father as well, if not a victim herself. Luis favored his grandmother during his childhood, and since she lived with them she was a ready source of shelter. Her death in his teenage years dealt him a blow from which he was still trying to recover. Beyond the abuse, Luis' father was swaggering and masculine in a way that I believed intimidated his sensitive son. Luis brought up memories of his father urinating with the door open in order to show him his much bigger penis. My Freudian senses noted the obvious implications. He also showed Luis violent movies and pornography well before he was ready to take in, much less understand, such things.

But that was not how he saw his father now. His father had become a broken, rather sad creature in retirement. His body was bent and fragile from years of manual labor, and he had settled into a routine that included his bed, his couch, his television, and not much else. Left with no one to dominate, he had sunk inward until there was little left of the abusive man he used to be.

Luis could remember the physical and emotional abuse well, but he feared that more had occurred. He often returned to his suspicion that he was sexually abused by his father. When I explored his evidence for this, he remembered his father being on top of him, the sensation of gasping for air, and little else. If only someone could come along and unlock these repressed memories for him, he said, he would finally be free. I was aware that Luis had expressed this belief to previous therapists as well, none of whom had made any progress in further uncovering the narrative.

To be absolutely clear, I still do not know whether or not Luis was molested by his father. I explained to him that repressed memories, and traumatic memories in general, do not work like narratives hidden away in a safe until the key can be found. Rather, they are sensory impressions of an experience: the tone of voice, the smell of cologne, the pressure of hands. Being as straightforward with him as possible, I told him that we could not get at the memories directly but could explore what it would mean for Luis both if they were true and if they were not.

In this phase of my work with Luis, I thought often of Winnicott's paper "Fear of Breakdown." Winnicott begins by noting the visceral fear some (but not all) patients have upon beginning treatment that they will at some point literally fall apart. He links this with earlier childhood fears, "primitive agonies," that include falling forever and disintegrating. He contends that such fears are *"the fear of a breakdown that has already been experienced."*[2] This fear of falling apart isn't something that occurs in the course of treatment but rather that which has already occurred and to which the patient has responded, and their response (their defense mechanisms, in psychoanalytic speak) are what bring them to treatment.

Luis's fears that his father had molested him were rooted in some real (and troubling) experiences, but his constant efforts to uncover the truth obscured the fact that several boundary violations occurred of which Luis was consciously aware. His father did not need to have molested him to have been a terrible, abusive presence and a negative influence in his development. Luis' search for even more trauma ran the risk of diminishing the trauma he remembered all too easily, carrying the implicit message that "merely" being physically abused was not sufficient to explain his current mental health struggles.

Luis' father loomed large over our treatment, but he was not the only factor that contributed to Luis' suffering. After we had been working together for a few months, Luis began a session with me by recounting how he had recently attended a reunion for former students of Whitney Young, one of the city's top selective enrollment high schools. By this point I felt fairly familiar with the contours of Luis' biography, but this took me by surprise. I wondered if Luis was testing me to see how much research I had really done on his background, but I felt it was better to admit my ignorance rather than plod ahead like I knew

Luis

what he was talking about. "I wasn't aware that you had attended Whitney Young," I said.

"Oh yeah, I went there for my freshman year. I just couldn't get my gym grade up though—the teacher really had it in for me—so I had to transfer back to my neighborhood high school for the other three years. I really loved going there, though, and I wish I had stayed."

———

Chicago Public Schools (CPS) offers a mixture of neighborhood high schools and eleven specialty schools that you must test into in order to attend. Admission for the latter can be tough; in 2018 less than a third who applied were selected at all,[3] and of those who were accepted only about 20 percent got into one of their top three picks.[4] Chicago's selective enrollment high schools are meant to be the crown jewels of the system, and they attract applicants from outside the city. Suburban families can apply for admission as long as they plan to move to the city (or find an address in the city to claim as their own) before the school year commences. Additionally, many private school students will make the transition to CPS if they are accepted into one of the top-tier schools. All told, about 15 percent of those accepted come from outside CPS. These high schools also have another crucial thing in common: They are very, very white in a majority-minority school district.

Currently, Chicago Public Schools as a whole is 47 percent Latinx, 37 percent Black, 10 percent White, and 4 percent Asian (plus smaller percentages of multiracial, Native American, and Pacific Islander students).[5] When the nonprofit Metropolitan Planning Council examined enrollment statistics at the top five selective enrollment high schools from 2000 to 2017, they found that over the years the total population was 33 percent Latinx, 13 percent Black, 35 percent White, and 14 percent Asian.[6] These schools have actually become less diverse since Luis briefly attended one; a consent decree which allowed race to be considered in admissions was lifted in 2009.

When not just race but socioeconomic status is taken into account, it becomes even more clear that selective enrollment high schools have and continue to fail low-income students such as Luis. According to a 2016 study by the University of Chicago Consortium on School Research, poor students are 13 percent less likely to be admitted to a selective college if they attended a selective enrollment school for high school when compared to their peers who attended neighborhood schools. The same does not hold true for well-off students; attending a selective enrollment high school boosts their chances of admission to a selective college by 11 percent. Upon closer inspection it becomes clear that CPS's selective enrollment high schools are mostly there for the few white and wealthy students who live in the district rather than the majority black and brown students who struggle to be admitted and often do not benefit from the education they receive there.

It was obvious to me why Luis would place so much stock in being an alumnus of Whitney Young no matter how brief his stay. Being admitted to the prestigious school was a real boost to him, and I imagine to the developing mind of an adolescent trying to move beyond an abusive household it represented a way out. The pain of failing, of having to return to peers who knew that you had tried to do better and didn't succeed, had to sting.

To be sure, selective enrollment schools should be more diverse and more supportive of students from a variety of backgrounds. At the same time, we must avoid the implicit narrative in discussing such schools that elevates their status at the expense of those in the neighborhood. Neighborhood schools are not the cesspools of despair as commonly depicted in narratives about public education; often they do as well or even better at preparing their students for college than selective enrollment high schools. Neighborhood schools look like the neighborhoods they serve, meaning students receive more peer support since their classmates live in the same neighborhood and most likely share the same socioeconomic status. These schools also play a critical role beyond serving their students; they often act as informal third places where community members can gather and meet one another, increasing their level of commitment to the success of their neighborhood.

The critical role that schools play in certain communities makes what the city did in 2013 all the more galling. That year, the second of Mayor Rahm Emmanuel's tenure, Chicago Public Schools announced a list of as many as 330 neighborhood schools that could be shuttered, eventually paring it down to 50.[7] The rationale was that these schools were failing their students so completely that only a teardown and rebuilding could fix the deep-seated issues. According to the then-CEO of Chicago Public Schools Barbara Byrd-Bennett, an Emanuel appointee who would later be convicted on corruption charges, "For too long, children in certain parts of our city have been cheated out of the resources they need to succeed in the classroom because they are trapped in underutilized schools. These underutilized schools are also under-resourced." In a pattern that echoed the previous year's closure of community mental heath clinics, the majority of the schools that were closed were located on Chicago's South and West Sides.

Luis was long gone from the hallways of Chicago Public Schools by the time any of this happened, of course, and as far as I know Luis has not been greatly bothered by the school closings. When I look at Luis, though, I see a school system that failed him. I imagine the excitement that must have came when he received word of his acceptance into Whitney Young, and I imagine the bitter taste of having to transfer to his neighborhood school for his sophomore year. Luis did graduate, and for a time he attended a local university. He did not complete his degree, and it became one of a host of projects he has abandoned over the years. He has talked about becoming a computer programmer, a pastor, even a therapist. I think he could be capable of great things if his mental health stabilized, but the system never gave him a chance. I can't help but think of the children like Luis who are similarly held back by the chaos of the city's current educational system.

The earlier we help someone who is sick, regardless of whether the illness is mental or physical, the better. There's a reason why we encourage regular preventative cancer screenings for those most at risk: Stage I cancer is often an annoyance, while stage IV cancer can be a death sentence. I believe there are no death sentences in mental health, but I also believe no one should have to suffer longer than necessary. With all the teachers, social workers, and other professional helpers Luis must have encountered in his brief time at Whitney Young, there should have been ample opportunity to address his issues. I know teachers are horribly overworked (I'm married to one of them), so I certainly do not blame them. Still, I can't help but wish someone took the time to ask him what was going on with him, or, even better, the institution itself had policies and procedures in place to help such students who were struggling.

It's not just Luis who prompts such thoughts. I see another patient, an African American woman named Joanna, who spent decades of her life drinking two bottles of vodka per day. By her own telling, she started when she was twelve and didn't stop until she was in her fifties and got tired of waking up hungover every morning. It took Joanna some time to warm up to me, but when she did we began to untangle her reasons for picking up the bottle. Joanna lived with her mother, father, and grandfather, and all three of them were alcoholics. When her mother got drunk, she was physically abusive. When her father and grandfather got drunk, they raped her. Throughout this living nightmare, Joanna went to school most of the time, only staying home when her injuries were easily visible and couldn't be explained away. She prepared her six younger siblings for school every day as well. By her reckoning, she was drunk for most of junior high and high school, trying desperately to numb the pain of her repeated abuse.

Schools are so much more than places where children learn. They provide two meals per day (free to children whose parents can't afford them), yearly dental and vision exams, mental health treatment for children who need it, and positive adult role models for children who may lack them at home. None of this happens by magic, though. The maximum class size allowed by Chicago Public Schools is twenty-eight for kindergarten through third grade and thirty-one for grades four through eight, yet 20 percent of students are currently in classrooms that exceed those limits.[8] The recommended ratio of students to social workers is 250 to 1,[9] yet CPS currently employs one social worker for every 1,200 children.[10] It's not that teachers and staff don't care, it's that they simply don't have the time nor the space needed to do their jobs.

As I mentioned, my wife is a teacher, so you may dismiss me as hopefully biased. I will freely admit that I am a product of the public school education system and firmly believe that it works. My wife has taught in the same neighborhood elementary school for twelve years. In the neighborhood where she teaches large families are fairly common, and she's been there long enough that she often has brothers, sisters, and cousins from the same families. There are few things that bring her more pleasure and contentment in her role than seeing these former students succeed years down the line or getting to teach the younger siblings of former students. Every time she thinks about other job opportunities, she remembers the families she has taught through the years and cannot bring herself to sever the connection with them. All children deserve that kind of commitment, and our public education system should do everything it can to foster and support them.

————————

From all appearances Luis received a fine education at his local high school, and he has remained in the neighborhood where he grew up. He continues to be my patient, although issues have occasionally arisen in our work together. Last year, he came in and told me he was no longer receiving his food stamps because he failed to return some necessary documentation. Extending the paperwork to me, he told me previous therapists had filled it out for him and asked me to do the same. I considered it, but by this point I knew him well and felt sure he could do it himself. I politely declined to help him, suggesting that prior therapists had done so in order to empower him to do it on his own but, since that didn't seem to have worked, it was best that we try something different.

During our next session, he was somewhat reserved. After silence had settled thickly into my office, I asked him to talk about whatever was at the top of his mind.

"I wonder how Michelle is doing in private practice," he said. "I bet that she charges quite a bit and doesn't take my insurance." Michelle was a previous therapist of his, the one with whom he felt he made the most progress. He also had an erotic fixation upon her and believed that she had used her sex appeal to goad him into improving his hygiene.

Noting the obvious subtext, I responded, "I sense that you're not feeling happy with how things are working out between us."

"I have something that I want to bring up, but I worry that you'll be mad at me."

"You really don't have to worry about that. Are you concerned about our discussion regarding your food stamps from two weeks ago?"

"Yeah . . . I was just thinking that I know you're busy and I'm sure that you see a lot of other clients and we only meet every other week, so maybe I'm just not a priority for you, maybe you don't have the time or the energy to really help me."

I had a sense this was coming, so I wasn't surprised. I reassured Luis that I did value him as a patient, that I enjoyed helping him and looked forward to our time together (which was true). I apologized for not making my reasoning explicit and shared why I thought it was best for him to do it on his own. I don't know if he agreed with my decision, but he at least came to understand it and not feel abandoned.

We haven't kissed, of course, but there was (and is) an intimacy formed between us. Luis was able to express his feelings and to challenge me, and I provided a safe space for him to do so. We learn about therapeutic modalities and evidence-based practices for best outcomes in graduate school and beyond, but the most curative part of my work is the fact that people can come talk to me and be heard. In the years I've done this work, I've come to realize how hard it is to really get someone to listen to you without judgment or a personal agenda. Listening is one of the best gifts we can give one another.

It took me several years to really get to know Luis. He usually presents as abundantly assertive, cocky even. He's told me repeatedly about how his romantic relationships have ended because he cannot find a woman who is his intellectual equal and eventually grows tired of dumbing down his vocabulary. When he's manic his grandiosity swells even further, usually something along the lines of how he has a special mandate to save the world. Beneath the bluster, though, Luis doesn't really believe any of this.

A funny thing about narcissism in general is that those who seem to inflate their egos the most often lack any true sense of self. That's why narcissists often surround themselves with people who tell them what they want to hear and shun those who attempt to check them: lacking an ego of their own, they need others to tell them how great they are to avoid the hole within. Narcissism is a defense mechanism, and not a very good one at that.

Luis' messy home life combined with his academic struggles left him in search of someone to tell him that he was worthwhile, valuable. Instead he felt ignored throughout his formative school years, eventually finding some sort of solace in his inflated sense of self. This may have kept him from confronting his own inner-most fears and the failures of the past, but it also prevented him from completing his college degree, having a lasting and fulfilling romantic relationship, or maintaining steady employment. His hoarding was just the latest in a long line of failed attempts to make himself worthwhile to others.

I believe Luis could still reach those goals he has dreamed of for so long. If I didn't I would no longer be a therapist. This doesn't mean that I cannot mourn his missed opportunities, though, the times when if someone had been there to help the course of his life could have been radically changed for the better. Children and adolescents need at least one person in their lives who believes in them without reservation. Often that is one or both of their parents, but for Luis and others like him that is not possible. Teachers can fill that role, but they aren't magic. That takes time too, time that is too often in short supply in an era of swelling classroom sizes, limited supports for teachers, and relentless focus from administrators on tangible things like test scores rather than student well-being.

Communities do not automatically become close and supportive just because people are geographically located near one another. They require meeting places, "third places" like schools or clinics that allow people to cross paths and interact. We often hear about food deserts when it comes to urban environments, and that is important; everyone needs access to good and healthy food. We're focusing our attention too narrowly, though. Alongside food deserts, we need to consider school deserts, community mental health deserts, and job deserts.

For too long conversations about violence in Chicago have

treated each individual gunshot as an isolated incident. Plenty of people live in poverty and are never violent, to be sure, and choosing to take a human life is a choice an individual makes on his or her own. At the same time, though, we can try to understand the factors that influence such decisions and do what we can to address the root causes, the historical traumas that have shaped communities for generations. A child who grows up attending a school in a different neighborhood where they don't know anyone and is forced to cross rival gang territories just to get to class, who has no access to mental health services when they need to talk to someone, who doesn't have people in the community who are invested in their lives and make sure that they know it is far more likely to grow up feeling hopeless and be at a greater risk for violence (either as perpetrator or victim).

There will always be people like myself to help the Luises of the world, those that slip through the cracks, but increasingly there are more Luises and less of people like me. Rather than focusing on the often-difficult work of repairing earlier traumas and gaps in care, we would save the world a lot of misery (and, frankly, money) if we worked to stop such problems before they started. We know that healthy communities help produce healthy children who grow into healthy adults. The question is whether we care enough or not to invest in communities like the one Luis calls home.

CHAPTER 5

ANTHONY

Knocking on the frame of my open door, one of my co-workers leaned in and said, "I have a new client for you. I just did his intake and I think he needs to talk to someone soon."

"Okay," I told her. "I'll set him up with an appointment."

"Are you free right now? Just for a few minutes. He really needs it. His name is Anthony, he's right out here in the waiting room. Let me introduce you."

Later I would find out the depths of Anthony's pain, but the moment he stepped into my office I could see he was suffering. He was wearing all black and his arms were coiled tightly around his core. He was in his early 40s but appeared much older, not just due to his thinning hair which he kept closely shaved. His eyes glanced at me suspiciously from behind his thick glasses. He was of an average height and weight but his posture made him seem much smaller. He largely kept to the same position over our first few sessions, but he did soften slightly the more we got to know each other.

Anthony was born to a father who was emotionally abusive and a mother who was overwhelmed. They had too many children, he told me, so his mother picked a few to send back to their native Mexico. Anthony was forced to move there when he was eight. He didn't know a word of Spanish. His paternal grandmother made him work in the fields and whipped him when he was disobedient. School became a distant memory. When he turned thirteen, his mother brought him back to the United States. He enrolled in school again but was hopelessly behind. He could not read or write, and he was discovering that he preferred to stay in the streets rather than go to school.

Anthony was in and out of juvenile institutions until he was seventeen. He got his girlfriend pregnant, and they got married when they were both eighteen. He tried to stay out of trouble and found a job working in a factory. Fortunately, he had a sympathetic supervisor that helped cover for him so no one would find out he was illiterate. Anthony had few allies at work; native Mexicans mocked his poor Spanish, and most of his other coworkers wrote him off as undocumented and therefore disposable. His supervisor retired, and his successor was not as kind. Anthony endured it for a few more years until he quit. He probably would have had to leave the job soon anyway. He had developed carpal tunnel syndrome, and his right hand remained claw-like and numb even following surgery. Around the time his job was falling apart, Anthony came home to discover his wife in bed with another man. He admitted that their relationship wasn't really working by this point, but he was still shocked. They divorced, and their three children who were now teenagers lived with their mother and visited Anthony on the weekend.

All of that would have been more than enough to leave its mark, and we certainly processed these events over time. But it was not the years of childhood abuse, the workplace harassment, or the divorce that Anthony needed to talk about the most. In his telling, his life had ended nine years ago.

It was his son's sixteenth birthday. They had plans to celebrate that evening, but during the day his son was wandering around the neighborhood and talking to his friends. Anthony hadn't seen him as much lately and was feeling worried as fathers do. His son was walking into a corner store a few blocks from his house when a minivan pulled up beside him. Three males barely older than him were inside. Words were exchanged. One of them jumped out of the van and shot his son in the head. He crumpled to the sidewalk, dying instantly.

When a child dies, you mourn not just the life that was lost but all of the life that could have been but now will never be. Anthony loved sports, but every time he sat down to watch a Bears game he remembered how he and his son used to watch them together. He thought about dating but then felt guilty about being with someone his son would never meet. As his daughters grew and experienced the heartaches and pains of adulthood, he wondered what sort of man his son would have been. It was tearing him apart.

———————————

I was walking through the security line in the Albuquerque airport recently when a TSA agent waved me over, pointing at our diaper bag. I wasn't sure what was in it that had set off the sensors, but it could have been one of any number of things. My daughter is in the habit of secretly stashing items inside its many pockets, so I hoped it wasn't something too egregious. It turned out that we had merely forgotten to empty her sippy cup, and the TSA agent offered to do a quick test on it so we didn't have to dump the water out. Knowing how hard it is to navigate the airport with a baby, I gladly consented, and while he was doing whatever he needed to do we made small talk.

"Where are you headed to?"

"Chicago. Home."

"Like Chicago Chicago, or the suburbs? I meet a lot of people who say they're from Chicago, but it turns out they actually live in the suburbs."

"No, we live in the city."

"Is that safe? I hear a lot about all of the murders and violence you guys have. Not a place I'd want to be."

"Yeah, we feel pretty safe. We really like our neighborhood."
"Oh. Well, good."

We stood awkwardly for a few beats, waiting for the test results. When the agent was satisfied, I thanked him for the help and moved on.

Exchanges like this are the reason I've hesitated to write further on Chicago and gun violence. "When you look at what's going on in Chicago. What the hell is going on in Chicago? What the hell is happening there?"[1] Donald Trump asked a recent class of graduating FBI recruits. When the city sued the Justice Department for trying to penalize sanctuary cities, Jeff Sessions replied in a statement, "Chicago needs . . . a recommitment to the rule of law and to policies that roll back the culture of lawlessness that has beset the city."[2] Fox News contributor and former Arkansas governor Mike Huckabee tweeted in 2017: "On way to Chicago for speech. Expecting to have to run from plane dodging bullets like Hillary did in Bosnia when under sniper fire! Yikes!"[3]

In 2016, Chicago's murder rate spiked from 485 to 764. Chicago's rapid increase mirrored an overall rise in homicides in many other major American cities.[4] The number dropped significantly in 2017 to 650, and decreased again in 2018 to 561. However, Chicago is also home to a well-developed network of urban hospitals skilled in trauma, which means these figures are actually lower than they could be given the number of gunshot victims.[5]

Numbers alone don't provide an adequate scope of the problem. Chicago is the third-most populous city in the nation (currently 2.7 million), but crime data from 2010 to 2015 shows that Chicago actually had the eighteenth highest per capita murder rate among cities with populations greater than 250,000.[6] The murder spike in 2016 pushed Chicago nearer the top of the list, but it is still well below other cities such as New Orleans, Detroit, St. Louis, and Baltimore.

Nevertheless, Chicago's murder rate remains troubling even if the prevailing narrative has uncomfortable racial undertones. Researchers and commentators have offered up a number of causes for the rapid rise in 2016. Some have blamed conflicts between rival gangs. Beginning in the mid-1990s, leaders of the Gangster's Disciples, the Vice Lords, the Black Disciples, and the Latin Kings were successfully prosecuted and incarcerated, and their once-fearsome gangs dissolved in their absence. Dozens, perhaps hundreds, of smaller gangs rose up to take their place. Instead of large-scale operations run by Stringer Bell–types, there are now cliques of mostly young men who band together to rule over their immediate surroundings. If you have four major gangs operating in the city, the number of conflicts regarding boundaries and territories is somewhat limited. If that number is much higher and membership defined more loosely, the potential for violence rises exponentially. Others have blamed the rise in violence on the so-called ACLU effect, citing a 2016 agreement between the CPD and the ACLU that reformed stop-and-frisk policies.[7] Street stops rarely have an impact upon violent crime rates, though, and the researchers who generated headlines by suggesting a causal link have also written that reading someone their Miranda rights places an unnecessary burden upon the police.[8] More rigorous analysis has suggested that murders rose due to a variety of factors, and a definitive answer to the question is most likely not available.[9]

Chicago had a violence problem before 2016. Our murder rate per capita is well above that of New York and Los Angeles and has been for years. The term "Chiraq" was first coined in 2009 by local rapper King Louie. While his intention was to capture the reality of his experience and the real dangers people of color face, the term quickly spread beyond the city limits to become a shorthand way of equating Chicago's violence with that in the destabilized Iraq. As "Chiraq" became the subject of a *Vice* documentary and the title of both a Nicki Minaj song and a Spike Lee film, the backlash from residents grew. Chance the Rapper responded to Lee's film by tweeting "That shit get ZERO love out here. Shit is goofy and it's a bunch of ppl from NOT around here telling u to support that shit . . . It's exploitive and problematic." Lee didn't win any fans in Chicago when he responded to Chance's critique by pointing out that his father had worked for Rahm Emanuel and criticized him for not being sufficiently critical of the mayor.

Thus far I have been treating Chicago as a single entity, but when it comes to the homicide rate, like so many other things, there are two Chicagos that rarely intersect. Twelve of the city's seventy-seven defined community areas had no murders in 2016, and five of those same areas on the city's South and West Sides were responsible for almost a third of the murders. In 2016, the murder rate per 100,000 people was 179.5 in Englewood and 148.3 in West Garfield Park,[10] significantly higher than Caracas, Venezuela, which topped the list of most dangerous cities in the world with 119.87 murders per 100,000 residents.

I cannot ignore Chicago's violence problem because it impacts the lives of my clients. Many of the therapeutic techniques I was taught in graduate school simply don't work in communities marred by pervasive trauma. I firmly believe that getting out into nature, whether that's going for a walk or sitting in a park, can be deeply therapeutic, but I always add the caveat "if that's safe for you in your neighborhood."

I hate the term "Chiraq" for the ways in which it's been co-opted by outsiders like Spike Lee and how it paints the city with a broad brush, but I know that many of my patients feel like they live in a war zone. Too many of them have told me about falling asleep to the sound of gunshots, of not letting their young children play outside for fear they will be caught in the crossfire, of the near-death experiences they have had at bus stops, funerals, and other places that we would expect to be safe. Violence has even come near my home: A few months ago someone was shot to death outside of a bar just a few blocks away. For a while I felt especially vigilant, but with the distance of time such memories fade. For most of my patients, though, violence is not a temporary aberration but rather a regular occurrence in their communities. They don't have the luxury of forgetting.

Our mental health diagnoses are inadequate for this level of trauma. The symptoms of posttraumatic stress disorder fit what a person experiences when a horrible incident shatters their world; they are less accurate when someone never had a safe and coherent vision of the world in the first place. Researchers have long been curious to see how the legacy of the Holocaust has been transmitted from survivors of concentration camps to their children who were born after the war, and over 500 studies have been published to analyze their functioning on a variety of levels. There is no direct line of causality, but these children were at a higher risk of PTSD even before they were exposed to a traumatic event.[11] For some this secondhand exposure to the evils of humankind increased their resiliency, but for others it increased their toxic stress and made them more susceptible to mental illness as well as a host of diseases and other forms of suffering.

I worry most about the children. Every random crossfire death is a tragedy, but we tend not to think about the many more children who are growing up in environments that feel profoundly unsafe to them, often despite the best efforts of their parents. Some will undoubtedly grow stronger and create beautiful, profound meaning out of the pain they have witnessed. Far more, though, will never know what it's like to not live in a world where they know they could die at any time and will have their own adult lives diminished as a result. In one of the more violent neighborhoods of Chicago, West Garfield Park, the average life expectancy is sixty-nine years, the same as in Iraq. That takes into account murders, of course, but also cancer, diabetes, and other illnesses that disproportionately impact the poor. If you hop on the Green

Line in West Garfield Park and travel downtown, a fifteen-minute ride that covers six miles, the average life expectancy shoots up to eighty-five.[12]

I did an intake once on a man a few years younger than myself who had lost most of his friends and a few of his family members to gun violence. I was doing all the things I normally do, gathering the relevant information while providing supportive feedback, when he looked up at me through tears and asked, "Have you ever lost anyone?" I was caught off-guard. I stammered that I had lost my a few great-grandparents, a grandpa to old age, and an aunt to cancer, but I knew that's not what he meant. I added, "No, I've never known anyone who has been murdered." He continued talking and I continued listening, but I knew that a small barrier had risen between us. I felt my privilege.

There is no quick fix treatment for trauma. Occasionally some new and exciting intervention will come to the fore and show some promise in clinical trials, but they are almost always designed for single incidents of trauma: car crashes, assaults, and the like. For those who have been steeped in trauma since their childhoods, it is not nearly so clear-cut. Judith Herman, a trauma-tologist whose book *Trauma and Recovery*[13] is a classic within the field, developed a stage-based model of trauma treatment that I utilize in my practice. The first task of the therapist is to make the client feel safe. Once this is accomplished (which can take months or even years), we then work on helping the client narrate the story of what happened to them. Finally, we focus on helping the client integrate their traumatic experiences into the narrative of their life, reconnecting to their history and to those around them.

This is the path that I took with Anthony. He cycled through a whole range of emotions when we first began working together:

anger at those who had hurt him in the past, frustration at his ex-wife whom he still blamed to some degree for their son's death, deep depression when thinking of how his family would never feel complete again. In one sense Anthony's experience was different than the majority of those in Chicago who have had loved ones murdered. His son's murderers were caught and put on trial. Only one out of every twenty murder cases results in a conviction.[14]

Anthony was able to see his son's murderers face-to-face at their trial. He still felt deep anger at what they had stolen from him, but he was also able to see that they too were young, not much older than his son. He was satisfied when they were convicted, but I don't think it helped as much as he had thought he might. One of the killers did flee, Anthony believed back to his native Mexico, and while I could tell how much this frustrated him it wasn't something that came up often in our sessions.

For most of the early days of our work together I just listened. I listened while Anthony shared his grief, listened as he reflected upon how his son's death had shattered his family, listened as he described his struggles with substance abuse following the murder. What can one say to someone undergoing one of the most heartbreaking losses a human being can experience? My training as a therapist hasn't given me any magic words that can make it better. They don't exist. One thing I have realized, though, is how profoundly uncomfortable most of us are with grief and loss. I think it's particularly hard in cases of senseless death because one can't help but think, "What if that was me?" I didn't yet have children when Anthony and I first started, which probably helped give me a bit of detachment from his reality. All the same, the most therapeutic thing I or anyone else can do when faced with such deep sorrow is listen and not turn away.

I believe it was easier for Anthony to integrate the story of his son's murder into his life because he knew what had happened. This can be a double-edged sword, to be sure. Still, Anthony was reassured that his son was not himself in a gang, derived some bit of comfort from the fact that it was terribly random.

Anthony's grief at his son's passing never went away. I often tell my patients that such loss is like experiencing the amputation of a limb—you grow to cope with your new reality but you are never without reminders of that which you have lost. So many of the things that we tell those who are grieving are more for our comfort than theirs. Anthony was religious, and he believed that his son was in a better place, but that did little to lessen the emotional pain.

As Anthony allowed his grief for his son to pour out, other pains rose to the fore as well. This can be a hard part of working with trauma: It often gets worse before it gets better. We work very hard to erect mental barriers around those elements of our past that hurt us, and while this is a poor long-term strategy it has some short-term effectiveness. If it didn't we would have stopped doing it long ago. Discussing such issues as they arise is a little like tearing off a Band-Aid—it's a necessary task once healing has begun, but it still hurts like hell.

Anthony had lost his apartment due both to the fog of grief and being unable to find a job that would hire him. When he had worked earlier, his wife had helped him fill out the necessary applications and was able to fake the rest of it, but as even low-paying jobs require a high school degree these days his options were quite limited. He sometimes helped a friend with odd jobs for a hundred bucks or so in cash a day when the work was available, but soon this friend stopped being so regular with paying him and then refused altogether. Anthony moved between the apartments of his mother and his daughter, though more often the former as his daughter had two small children to care for.

Anthony's resentment of his mother began to grow as he progressed in treatment. Questions that he had buried began to arise in his mind: Why did he have to go to Mexico and not one of his brothers? Why did she let his father verbally abuse him? Why hadn't she pushed him to go to school? Anthony asked all of these questions of her regularly, and her answer was usually something along the lines of, "That was in the past, you should forget about it and move on." Anthony didn't, and I think there was something therapeutic about his anger. I didn't want him to bully his mother, of course, and I don't think he ever did. Still, I think asking "why" and waiting for a real answer helped him express feelings towards her that he had long-buried in his attempt to be a dutiful son. We typically associate "why" questions with young children learning to be curious about their world and the whole notion of causality. I think Anthony's questions allowed him to return to that time, to ask his mother the questions he didn't have a voice for back then and in the process to overcome a developmental impasse.

Anthony never got the answer that he wanted from these questions, and I'm not sure such an answer exists anyway. He did learn to be comfortable with his questions and to hold both his present experience and his regrets in tension. He still thought of his son while watching football games, but he was able to both feel grief for his loss and enjoy the game, at least for most of it. After a long struggle, he also began to receive disability benefits. Although the amount he received each month was quite meager, having any kind of income allowed him to reclaim some small measure of self-respect.

When Anthony and I wrapped up our work, he had recently moved into an apartment in his old neighborhood. Before he received Social Security he would often talk about moving away to somewhere like Florida, far from the painful memories associated with Chicago. But his granddaughters were also here, and he enjoyed walking them to and from school every day. His route took him near where his son had been killed, and while this was difficult at first, the pain faded somewhat over time. He marveled at his own ability to cope.

Anthony took his mother into his new apartment along with one of his brothers who was down on his luck. This arrangement wasn't perfect; some of the same tensions were present. This switch from the cared-for to the caregiver was an important milestone for Anthony, though. His self-image as needy and broken fell away as he found real meaning in caring for his mother in the last years of her life.

There are a lot of Anthonys in Chicago. There are also a lot of residents who lacked some of the necessary supports he had, who had to contend with unsolved murders, few family members, and no money. And, of course, there are plenty of people like me here too who hear about violence on the news and maybe have a shooting in their neighborhood once or twice a year. Which camp you fall into is often a matter of where you can afford to live.

CONCLUSION

I remember the first time I came into contact with the sort of community trauma I've been discussing here. It was before I even started my social work degree; I was in seminary at the time and had recently begun an internship at a church on Chicago's West Side. I mostly met with people in the community and spoke to residents of their residential drug and alcohol recovery program. One evening I received a call from my supervisor.

"Make sure and wear a suit tomorrow," he said. "We're going to have a funeral."

I had been to funerals for infants already as part of the placement, so I didn't expect it to be much different. The deceased was a black man, younger than myself by a few years. I didn't probe the details, but I knew he had been shot nearby. My supervisor asked me to offer the opening prayer, and although I felt inadequate to the task I managed to do it. As I took my seat on the stage, the other pastors led the rest of the service. The one who knew him best gave the sermon, recounting the deceased's life and bemoaning the cost of violence. It was personalized and sincere, but I got the impression that he had given this sermon many times before.

When he finished, those who had gathered began offering their memories of the deceased. I watched as a steady succession of people, most in their teens and twenties, spoke through bitter tears about his life. It didn't seem to end, and with each breakdown at the microphone the heaviness in the room fell even further upon all of our shoulders. I remember looking at his mother, who was sitting stoic in the front row. She bestowed hugs on everyone as they walked back to their seat, offering them reassurances that he was in a better place now. She maintained her composure until people began walking by the casket for the final viewing.

She went last. When she saw his face, knowing it was the final time, she fell apart. She screamed and cried, falling upon his body. Over and over, she yelled at him, "I told you not to go there that night! I told you not to go there that night!" She continued for what felt like an eternity, even as other family members came up to flank her on both sides. When she was too tired to continue they escorted her back to her chair. She dropped into it heavily, her body still racked by sobs.

I had never been in the presence of so much raw grief. I felt it hanging like a cloud above our heads, the pain and the rage and the hurt all swirling together. As people finally began filing out, my supervisor and I talked.

"Wow, that was really hard," I told him.

"Yeah, ones like these usually are," he responded. "We have another one coming up in a few days, same situation."

If you spend much time in community mental health, or social work in general, two phrases pop up with regularity: "vicarious trauma" and "compassion fatigue." The textbook in my first social work class described the symptoms of vicarious trauma as follows: "decreased energy; lack of self-time; disconnecting from loved ones; social withdrawal; increased sensitivity to violence, threats, or fear; cynicism, generalized despair, and hopelessness."[1] Compassion fatigue is closely related; over time it gets hard to soak up the pain of others, and at a certain point you just get tired of it.

Lisa McCann and Laurie Ann Pearlman, two clinicians at the Traumatic Stress Institute in New Britain, CT, first wrote about the concept of vicarious trauma in a 1990 article.[2] According to them, during sessions the experiences of the patient confront the schemas of the therapist, the beliefs about the world the therapist has (mostly unknowingly) developed to help make sense of life. We all have core schemas that are rooted deep within us: people are truthful, I am safe, the world is a good place. If someone or something challenges these schemas with an opposing narrative drawn from their own experience the therapist could begin to develop the symptoms described above.

You may have noticed that the symptoms of vicarious trauma seem to mirror those of posttraumatic stress disorder. Indeed, the mechanism of vicarious trauma works by the therapist introjecting (drawing into himself) the trauma of the client and thereby experiencing many of the same symptoms. Vicarious trauma, then, is a sort of PTSD for people's stories, and compassion fatigue is often the result.

Vicarious trauma is the dominant paradigm for describing how this sort of work can impact a mental health professional. We discussed it in my very first class at graduate school, the accreditation requirements of my clinic require me to attend a yearly training on it, and once a month we devote the entirety of our staff meeting to sharing what we have been hearing from our patients and how it has impacted us. When I began this work as an intern I was convinced that vicarious trauma lurked around the corner and was hypervigilant for any manifestation of the symptoms.

I did change. If a car drove past me slowly when I was out walking my dog I would flinch, remembering the stories I had heard where shots burst forth from unseen assailants behind the wheel. I became more hesitant to leave the house after dark. I stopped biking to my classes because every available route passed through a neighborhood home to an increased number of shootings.

I did not grow up here. I was born in the western suburbs, but my parents moved about three hours downstate when I was six months old. I grew up in a town of only about five hundred people;

the size of my graduating class was forty-two. My grandfather was the area's appliance repairman, so even if people didn't know who I was they would if I told them I was Ken Stanberry's grandson. Whatever violence existed in that community was an aberration. When I was eleven, there was a triple homicide within the school district, and while I remember being scared in a general way it didn't really threaten my sense of safety. I grew up with many of those same schemas vulnerable to vicarious trauma: I thought the world was mostly a good and safe place, that people were kind to each other, that when wrong occurred it would be punished appropriately. Has my work irreducibly shattered such notions? Yes and no.

As I've grown older, both as a person and as a therapist, I have become more aware of the deep hurt that we can do to one another, of the unfortunate pervasiveness of childhood trauma, the reality of mass incarceration, the ways that systematic disinvestment and implicit narratives of white supremacy have decimated many urban areas across America. That is of course traumatizing, but it's also the experience of the patients I treat. It's an unfortunate reality of the work I do that most of the people who perform such services are white and from relatively privileged backgrounds while the people we serve are more often poor people of color. One highly-cited study found an increased prevalence of trauma-related symptoms in social workers who work in settings similar to my own, but the average respondent had a mean age of 45.7 years, was female (88.5 percent), and was Caucasian (75.2 percent).[3] There are clearly other factors at play here.

There is something that changes in you by doing this work. You grow to see the world in a different way, to have some of your sunnier convictions distilled by experience. I'm not convinced that vicarious trauma is the best way to talk about this, though. By retaining the connection to posttraumatic stress disorder there is a subtle but noticeable emphasis upon the person inflicting the trauma. I've worked with an innumerable amount of clinicians, almost all of whom care deeply for their clients and want the best for them. If we see our clients as potential sources of trauma, though, this can't help but shift the way that we approach them. Suddenly they seem somewhat dangerous, overwhelmingly needy.

This is all the more distressing when we consider this is how most of society already sees my patients. We're all familiar with the standard conservative talking points about the very poor who receive benefits, however meager, from the government. The right routinely depicts them as both a burden and a threat to the rest of "us." We can't forget, though, that welfare was gutted not by a Republican but a Democrat, the same president who put mass incarceration on steroids through his crime bill. Both parties have failed the urban poor. Both consistently fail to consider their unique perspective and needs when it comes to policy.

Have my experiences changed my schemas about the world? Absolutely. Perhaps you've felt something similar as you've read through these pages. Most of us have structured our lives to avoid the stories of people like Jacqueline, Frida, Robert, Luis, and Anthony. If we do run across them it is usually as a statistic on the evening news, perhaps a brief bit of local color in a piece by a journalist who parachuted in over a weekend to chronicle the "real" Chicago. It is uncomfortable to sit with pain, and most of us would rather avoid it if we could. And we do.

I did not write this book to make people feel miserable. If you walk away from reading this and only remember the tragedies, you're missing at least half the story. I do not choose to work in this field and at this clinic out of some masochistic urge to wallow in the pain of others. I am deeply bothered by the injustices I see on a daily basis, yes, but it goes deeper than that. Vicarious trauma ultimately fails because it only tells part of the story.

Some therapists and others in the helping professions speak about a twin phenomenon of vicarious trauma, vicarious resilience. The idea of vicarious resilience is that working with patients who have seen so much and yet manage to keep on moving can be inspiring, hopeful. Seeing how much another human being can bear and yet remain standing can make us marvel at what humans can accomplish. In my experience, such moments are often smaller than the trauma but even more crucial. I think of Frida working out a visitation schedule for her children and planning what they will do together, of Robert's burgeoning essential oils business, of Anthony caring for his mother.

Focusing on resilience can be dangerous in its own right. Think of the genre of college application essays that offer some version of "I went to (insert developing country) to help, but really it was me who was helped by them." My patients don't exist to provide uplifting stories for others' benefit any more than they are there to bring them down with stories of what they've endured.

The reaction required from those of us who don't share the situations of my patients (and I'm guessing that's most of my readers) is twofold. Yes, marvel at their ability to pull through, to make something despite the odds stacked against them. Most of them feel hopeful about their futures, so there is no reason we shouldn't as well. For those of us who have played a part in creating and sustaining the structures that make them miserable, though, we have to do more than simply praise their strength. We need to ask the hard questions about what created and often sustains their misery. Community trauma isn't something that arrives out of nowhere.

Why is the mental health establishment of which I am a part often so ill-equipped to treat minority populations? Why is the Department of Child and Family Services so broken? Why has the Chicago Housing Authority been unable to provide basic shelter to its citizens for decades even as it has record amounts of money in the bank? Why do Chicago Public Schools so often fail their students? What made Chicago so violent? These same questions could be asked of any major American city. An answer to just one of these questions would easily fill a book, and I don't pretend to offer a comprehensive solution to any one of these issues in the space provided here.

If we accept the premise that each of these systems was created mostly by middle-class whites to serve the needs of middle-class whites, everything begins to fall into place. White supremacy isn't just about those who wear white hoods and burn crosses. Most of the institutions I've written about here were created in a era when it was just assumed that whites were the superior race and the American culture should be built around them because it belonged to them. Thankfully fewer and fewer people believe this now, but we remain stuck with this sorrowful legacy and must take active steps to demolish it if we want a more just and equitable future.

My experience has been vastly different from that of my patients mostly due to the color of my skin and the amount of money my parents made. The prevailing Horatio Alger myth that we make ourselves and our futures simply isn't true. For every self-made man (or woman) there are many others who tried and failed as well as thousands of others who never even had the chance. The poor were seen as both a nuisance and a moral evil by the Puritans who founded this country, and even though we've shed their theology we continue to hold onto their myth of self-reliance.

How can we shed this false stigma? It starts with exercising our rights as citizens to support policies that actually address social and cultural disparities. We also need to bring positive political energy back into our communities, to create solidarity with the poor and fight against the powers that would render them invisible. When Martin Luther King, Jr., was assassinated, he was in the midst of a Poor People's Campaign. King had noticed the gains of the Civil Rights Movement but also believed that racial justice could only proceed so far without economic justice. He assembled a multiracial coalition to protest the condition of the poor in America, creating a unified group who had never identified with one another before. King and his coalition developed the following

Economic Bill of Rights: the right to full-employment that paid a living wage, the right to a minimum income, the right to a decent home in the neighborhood where one wishes to reside, the right to an adequate education, the right to participate in government and have one's voice and perspective honored, and the right to good healthcare. King's draft of these demands, written less than two months before he was murdered, ends with these words: "without these rights, neither the black and white poor, and even some who are not poor, can really possess the inalienable rights to life, liberty, and the pursuit of happiness. With these rights, the United States could, by the two hundredth anniversary of its Declaration of Independence, take giant steps towards redeeming the American dream."[4]

We've missed King's goal, but that's no reason to stop trying. Mental health issues do not occur in a vacuum; they are influenced by and often triggered by our experiences. The bifurcation between mental and physical health is a relic of an earlier time that separated the mind from the body. What happens in and to the body shapes the mind and vice versa. Would my patients experience the same symptoms if they had not been born poor people of color on Chicago's South and West Sides? In some cases it's doubtful. Others may have experienced some symptoms that could be quickly addressed by ready access to care.

I've invited you into my work to introduce you to those experiencing mental illness, both the struggles and the joys they experience. If you can put this down and forget all about them I haven't done my job. King's vision still cries out to be realized. We need nothing less than a modern-day Poor People's Movement to aid up those who by circumstance of their birth are at a higher likelihood of experiencing suffering in all its forms. This may be uncomfortable for some, but the health, even the very idea, of our democracy depends upon it. We know what we need to change. History will judge us on how we respond.

ACKNOWLEDGMENTS

Many thanks to Anne Trubek, Martha Bayne, Dan Crissman, and the rest of the staff at Belt Publishing and Belt Magazine. A few years ago I pitched the magazine a story about a lynching near my hometown that I had been mulling for ages and began the most fruitful relationship of my writing career. I'm grateful they took a chance on me for this project, and also thankful to be published by a small press dedicated to highlighting the region so dear to me.

To my parents, Cindy and Duane Askins and Neil and Patty Foiles. You provided space for me to explore my commitment to social justice which was kicked off by John Grisham novels and U2 albums (yes, I know). Thanks also to my wife's family who have always treated me as one of their own, Juan and Suzanne Angulo and the late William Crum. And, of course, my siblings (both biological and in-law): Christy Minnis, William Angulo, and Abigail Angulo.

I will remain forever indebted to Catherine Ortiz who accepted me as an intern when I showed up 15 minutes late for my first interview, frantic and sweating from the bike ride over. I've also had the pleasure of working with many other fantastic clinicians here, and I owe gratitude to many who have helped me best serve the patients I discuss.

I've been lucky to be the internship supervisor for the past few years, and if you will forgive the cliche I've learned as much from them as they (hopefully) have from me. I'm sure that

Kate McGinnis, Haijia Liu, Kendrick Dewdney, and Lauren Bernard will all become fantastic therapists--you're most of the way there already.

I deeply loved my graduate school experience at the University of Chicago School of Social Service Administration and my appreciation for what I learned there has only grown with time. I owe an extra debt of gratitude to the professors who first introduced me to the psychodynamic thinkers who people these pages, Bill Borden and the late Jason McVicker.

I don't think I would be able to offer the insights into the patients contained here if I had not had the guidance and mentorship of Julia Brown during the first two years of my clinical work. Our biweekly sessions were more than worth the time carved out of my day off. I am honored to be a part of the community that is the Chicago Center for Psychoanalysis.

None of this would have been possible without my wonderful wife Esther. Thanks for listening to me as I've thought through everything in these pages. You're a wonderful spouse, mother, and first draft reader. When I signed the contract for this book Elena Simone was an infant; now she's running around our house on her own two feet and chattering away. When I read these pages I am always reminded of how you grew up through the writing of it. It's an honor to be your father. Your smiling face when I get home from work is the best self-care I could ever find. This book is dedicated to both of you with all my love.

ENDNOTES

Introduction

1. Winston W. Shen, "A History of Antipsychotic Drug Development," *Comprehensive Psychiatry* 40, no. 6 (Nov.-Dec. 1999): 407-414.

2. Francisco López-Muñoz & Cecilio Alamo, "Monoaminergic Neurotransmission: The History of the Discovery of Antidepressants from 1950s Until Today," *Current Pharmaceutical Design* 15 (2009): 1563-1586.

3. "The State of Mental Health in America," Mental Health America, accessed November 7, 2018, http://www.mentalhealthamerica.net/issues/state-mental-health-america.

4. Mike Maciag, "Spotlight Shifts to Mental Health and States' Funding Cuts," *Governing,* December 20, 2012, http://www.governing.com/blogs/by-the-numbers/state-mental-health-funding-costs-and-budgets.html.

5. "Designated Health Professional Shortage Area Statistics: Fourth Quarter of Fiscal Year 2018 Designated HPSA Quarterly Summary As of September 30, 2018," Bureau of Health Workforce, Health Resources and Services Administration, and U.S. Department of Health and Human Services," accessed November 7, 2018, https://ersrs.hrsa.gov/ReportServer?/HGDW_Reports/BCD_HPSA/BCD_HPSA_SCR50_Qtr_Smry_HTML&rc:Toolbar=false.

6. Char Daston & Daniel Tucker, "A Look at the State of Mental Health Services in Chicago," *WBEZ,* October 11, 2018, https://www.wbez.org/shows/morning-shift/a-look-at-the-state-of-mental-health-services-in-chicago/92906829-9e18-46a6-959d-24ed3cb287d5.

7. Molly F. Gordon et. al., "School Closings in Chicago: Staff and Student Experiences and Academic Outcomes," *University of Chicago Consortium on School Research*, May 2018, https://consortium.uchicago.edu/sites/default/files/publications/School%20Closings%20in%20Chicago-May2018-Consortium.pdf.

8. Matt Ford, "What's Causing Chicago's Homicide Spike?," *The Atlantic,* January 24, 2017, https://www.theatlantic.com/politics/archive/2017/01/chicago-homicide-spike-2016/514331/.

9. See, e.g., Reuben J. Miller & Forrest Stuart, "Carceral Citizenship: Race, Rights and Responsibility in the Age of Mass Supervision," Theoretical Criminology 21, no. 4 (2017), 532-548.

10. American Psychiatric Association, *Diagnostic and Statistical Manual of Mental Disorders, Fifth Edition* (Arlington, VA: American Psychiatric Association, 2013).

11. "Social Determinants of Health: Know What Affects Health," Centers for Disease Control and Prevention, accessed November 7, 2018, https://www.cdc.gov/socialdeterminants/.

12. See, e.g., Jennifer A. Dean & Kathi Wilson, "'Education? It is irrelevant to my job now. It makes me very depressed…': exploring the health impacts of under/unemployment among highly skilled recent immigrants in Canada," Ethnicity & Health 14, No. 2 (April 2009), 185-204.

13. For an excellent overview see Hillary A. Franke, "Toxic Stress: Effects, Prevention, and Treatment," Children 1, no. 3 (Dec. 2014), 390-402.

Chapter 1

1. Michael Bennett & Sarah Bennett, *F*ck Feelings: One Shrink's Practical Advice for Managing All Life's Impossible Problems* (New York: Simon & Schuster, 2015), 213-214.

2. Ehud Bodner et. al., "The Attitudes of Psychiatric Hospital Staff Toward Hospitalization and Treatment of Patients with Borderline Personality Disorder," *BMC Psychiatry* 15, no. 2 (January 2015), 1-12.

3. Randy A. Sansone & Lori A. Sansone, "Gender Patterns in Borderline Personality Disorder," Innovations in Clinical Neuroscience 8, no. 5 (May 2011), 16-20.

4. Nadia Cattane et. al., "Borderline Personality Disorder and Childhood Trauma: Exploring the Affected Biological Systems and Mechanisms," *BMC Psychiatry* 17, no. 221, 1-14.

5. "Violence Against the Transgender Community in 2017," Human Rights Campaign, accessed August 31, 2018, https://www.hrc.org/resources/violence-against-the-transgender-community-in-2017.

6. Elyssa Cherney, "Chicago Homicide Victim Identified as Second Transgender Woman Killed in 6 Months," *Chicago Tribune,* February 23, 2017, http://www.chicagotribune.com/news/local/breaking/ct--tiara-richmond-transgender-woman-killed20170223-story.html.

7. Steven Jackson & Jason Nargis, "Making Chicago's Boystown," *WBEZ*, May 7, 2017, https://interactive.wbez.org/curiouscity/makingboystown/.

8. Terrence McCoy, "597 Days. And Still Waiting.", Washington Post, November 20, 2017, https://www.washingtonpost.com/sf/local/2017/11/20/10000-people-died-waiting-for-a-disability-decision-in-the-past-year-will-he-be-next/?utm_term=.a7a21f34cabb.

9. "TransLife Care: The Need & Our Response," Chicago House, accessed August 31, 2018, http://www.chicagohouse.org/wp-content/uploads/2013/12/Need-and-Response.pdf.

10. See, e.g., Enrique C. Leira, David C. Hess, & James C. Torner, "Rural-Urban Differences in Acute Stroke Management Practices: A Modifiable Disparity," *Neurological Review* 65, no. 7 (July 2008): 887-891.

11. Cathleen E. Willging, Melina Salvador, & Miria Kano, "Pragmatic Help Seeking: How Sexual and Gender Minority Groups Access Mental Health Care in a Rural State," *Psychiatric Services* 57, no. 6 (June 2006): 867-870.

12. Dejun Su et. al., "Mental Health Disparities Within the LBGT Population: A Comparison Between Transgender and Nontransgender Individuals," *Transgender Health* 1, no. 1 (2016): 12-20.

Chapter 2

1. Melanie Klein, "Notes on Some Schizoid Mechanisms," The International Journal of Psychoanalysis 27 (1946), 99-110.

2. William Borden, Contemporary Psychodynamic Theory and Practice (Chicago: Lyceum Books, 2009), 67.

3. Rich Miller, "Our Collapsing Social Services Net," *Capitol Fax*, May 15, 2017, https://capitolfax.com/2017/05/15/our-collapsing-social-services-net/.

4. For the following account see John E.B. Myers, *A History of Child Protection in America* (Bloomington, IN: Xlibris, 2004).

5. Richard Wexler, "The Children's Crusade," *Chicago Reader,* March 23, 1995, https://www.chicagoreader.com/chicago/the-childrens-crusade/Content?oid=887001.

6. Sam Charles, "Children in Care of DCFS at Lowest Point in 27 Years," *Chicago Sun-Times,* July 5, 2017, https://chicago.suntimes.com/news/children-in-care-of-dcfs-at-lowest-point-in-27-years/.

7. Gary Marx & David Jackson, "Illinois Lawmakers Seek DCFS Data about the Caseloads of Child Welfare Investigators," *Chicago Tribune,* September 26, 2017, http://www.chicagotribune.com/news/watchdog/ct-dcfs-lawmakers-caseloads-met-20170926-story.html.

8. David Jackson, Gary Marx, & Duaa Eldeib, "DCFS Investigators Competed for $100 Gift Cards for Closing Most Cases," *Chicago Tribune,* May 30, 2017, http://www.chicagotribune.com/news/local/breaking/ct-dcfs-contest-met-20170526-story.html.

9. "Racial Disproportionality and Disparity in Child Welfare," Child Welfare Information Gateway, accessed August 31, 2018, https://www.childwelfare.gov/pubpdfs/racial_disproportionality.pdf.

10. "Child Abuse and Neglect Statistics: Fiscal Year 2015 (Data as of January 31, 2016)," Illinois Department of Children and Family Services, accessed August 31, 2018,

https://www2.illinois.gov/dcfs/aboutus/newsandreports/Documents/DCFS_Annual_
Statistical_Report_FY2015.pdf.

11. Alan J. Dettlaff, "Disproportionality of Latino Children in Child Welfare,"
in *Challenging Racial Disproportionality in Child Welfare,* ed. Deborah K. Green
(Washington, D.C.: Child Welfare League of America Press, 2011), 119-129.

12. Jesse Rio Russell, Colleen Kerwin, & Julie L. Halverson, "Is Child Protective
Services Effective?," *Children and Youth Services Review* 84 (2018), 185-192.

13. Donald Winnicott, *Playing and Reality* (London: Routledge Classics, 2005).

14. Kate Thayer, "Wilmette Mom Investigated for Letting 8-Year-Old Walk Dog Around
the Block. 'For Something Like This to Happen to Me,' There's Something Really
Wrong," *Chicago Tribune,* August 23, 2018, http://www.chicagotribune.com/lifestyles/
ct-life-leaving-kids-alone-moms-shamed-20180820-story.html.

Chapter 3

1. For the history of Cabrini-Green, and of the CHA in general, see Ben Austen,
High-Risers: Cabrini-Green and the Fate of American Public Housing (New York:
Harper, 2018).

2. "Horrorella Talks Tolstoy, Beethoven and Candyman with Writer-Director Bernard
Rose!," Ain't It Cool News, August 12, 2015, http://www.aintitcool.com/node/72689

3. Audrey Petty (ed.), *High Rise Stories: Voices from Chicago Public Housing* (San
Francisco: McSweeney's, 2013).

4. Natalie Moore, "Why the Chicago Housing Authority Failed to Meet Its Mixed-
Income Ambitions," *WBEZ,* March 23, 2017, http://interactive.wbez.org/cha/.

5. Jason Grotto, "Chicago Housing Authority Stockpiles Cash, Pays Debts as Families
Languish on Waiting List," *Chicago Tribune,* January 13, 2017, http://www.chicagotribune.
com/news/local/breaking/ct-cha-finances-report-met-20170112-story.html.

6. Fran Spielman, "Under Fire for Removing Homeless from Lower Wacker, Emanuel Turns to Tiny Homes," June 8, 2018, https://chicago.suntimes.com/news/homeless-lower-wacker-emanuel-tiny-homes/.

7. Jacques Lacan, *The Seminar of Jacques Lacan Book III: The Psychoses 1955-1956,* trans. Russell Grigg (New York: W.W Norton & Co., 1997).

8. Annie Rogers, *The Unsayable: The Hidden Language of Trauma* (New York: Ballantine Books, 2006).

9. Ralph Waldo Emerson, "Nature."

Chapter 4

1. The Freud Reader, ed. Peter Gay (New York: W.W. Norton & Co., 1989), 309-350.

2. Winnicott, *Psycho-Analytic Explorations* (Cambridge, MA: Harvard University Press, 1989).

3. Juan Perez Jr., "Competition Remains Fierce for Top Programs as CPS Sends Out High School Offers," *Chicago Tribune*, March 30, 2018, http://www.chicagotribune.com/news/ct-met-chicago-high-school-application-offer-20180330-story.html.

4. Lauren FitzPatrick, "One in Five Applicants to Selective CPS High Schools Got a Top Three Choice," *Chicago Sun-Times*, March 30, 2018, https://chicago.suntimes.com/education/cps-8-out-of-every-10-eighth-graders-got-1-of-their-top-3-high-school-choices/.

5. "CPS Stats and Facts," Chicago Public Schools, Accessed August 31, 2018, https://cps.edu/About_CPS/At-a-glance/Pages/Stats_and_facts.aspx.

6. Alden Loury, "Data Points: Black Students Declining at Chicago's Top Public High Schools and in CPS Overall," *Metropolitan Planning Council,* August 31, 2017, https://www.metroplanning.org/news/8473/Data-Points-Black-students-declining-at-Chicagos-top-public-high-schools-and-in-CPS-overall.

7. For an in-depth look at the school closings and how they impacted students and families, see Eve L. Ewing, *Ghosts in the Schoolyard: Racism and School Closings on Chicago's South Side* (Chicago: University of Chicago Press, 2018).

8. Better Government Association, "Public Eye: 1 in 5 CPS Elementary Students Starts in Overcrowded Classrooms," *Chicago Sun-Times*, June 24, 2016, June 24, 2016, https://chicago.suntimes.com/news/public-eye-1-in-5-cps-elementary-students-starts-in-overcrowded-classrooms/.

9. National Association of Social Workers, "NASW Highlights the Growing Need for School Social Workers to Prevent School Violence," March 27, 2018, https://www.socialworkers.org/News/News-Releases/ID/1633/NASW-Highlights-the-Growing-Need-for-School-Social-Workers-to-Prevent-School-Violence.

10. Lauren FitzPatrick & Yvonne Kim, "CPS to Add Social Workers, Case Managers, But Not Enough for CTU," *Chicago Sun-Times*, July 16, 2018, https://chicago.suntimes.com/news/cps-to-add-social-workers-case-managers-but-not-enough-for-ctu/.

Chapter 5

1. Associated Press, "Trump Speaks About Chicago's Violence at FBI Training Graduation," WGN, December 15, 2017, https://wgntv.com/2017/12/15/trump-speaks-about-chicagos-violence-at-fbi-training-academy-graduation/.

2. "Statement by Attorney General Sessions on the City of Chicago's Lawsuit Against the U.S. Department of Justice," The United States Department of Justice, accessed November 13, 2018, https://www.justice.gov/opa/pr/statement-attorney-general-sessions-city-chicago-s-lawsuit-against-us-department-justice.

3. Mike Huckabee, "On way to Chicago for speech. Expecting to have to run from plane dodging bullets like Hillary did in Bosnia when under sniper fire! Yikes!," May 16, 2017, 1:52 PM, https://twitter.com/GovMikeHuckabee/status/864584262762336258.

4. "Murder Rates in 50 American Cities," *The Economist,* Accessed August 31, 2018, https://www.economist.com/graphic-detail/2017/02/07/murder-rates-in-50-american-cities.

5. Eric Ferkenhoff & Darnell Little," "The Bleeding of Chicago," *CityLab*, February 24, 2018, https://www.citylab.com/equity/2018/02/the-bleeding-of-chicago/554141/.

6. Francesca Mirabile, "Chicago Isn't Even Close to Being the Gun Violence Capital of the United States," *The Trace,* October 21, 2016, https://www.thetrace.org/2016/10/chicago-gun-violence-per-capita-rate/.

7. Paul G. Cassell & Richard Fowles, "What Caused the 2016 Chicago Homicide Spike? An Empirical Examination of the 'ACLU Effect' and the Role of Stop and Frisks in Preventing Gun Violence," *University of Illinois Law Review* (vol. 2018, no. 5).

8. Jeremy Gorner," "Study Blames 'ACLU Effect' for Spike in Chicago's Violence in 2016, But Experts Differ," *Chicago Tribune,* March 26, 2018, http://www.chicagotribune.com/news/local/breaking/ct-met-chicago-violence-2016-aclu-effect-20180315-story.html.

9. "Gun Violence in Chicago, 2016," University of Chicago Crime Lab, Accessed August 31, 2018, http://urbanlabs.uchicago.edu/attachments/store/2435a5d4658e2ca19f4f225b810ce0dbdb9231cbdb8d702e784087469ee3/UChicagoCrimeLab+Gun+Violence+in+Chicago+2016.pdf.

10. Ibid.

11. Natan Kellerman, "Transmitted Holocaust Trauma: Curse or Legacy? The Aggravating and Mitigating Factors of Holocaust Transmission," *The Israel Journal of Psychiatry and Related Sciences* 45 (2008), 263-270.

12. Nissa Rhee, "A Second City," *Chicago Magazine,* February 2018, http://www.chicagomag.com/city-life/February-2018/A-Second-City-West-Side-Health-Life-Expectancy/.

13. Judith Herman, *Trauma and Recovery: The Aftermath of Violence -- From Domestic Abuse to Political Terror* (New York: Basic Books, 2015).

14. Annie Sweeney & Jeremy Gorner, "Chicago Police Solve One in Every 20 Shootings. Here's Are Some Reasons Why That's So Low," *Chicago Tribune*, August 8, 2018, http://www.chicagotribune.com/news/local/breaking/ct-met-chicago-violence-clearance-rate-20180807-story.html.

Conclusion

1. Dean H. Hepworth et. al., *Direct Social Work Practice: Theory & Skills,* 9th ed. (Belmont, CA: Brooks/Cole CENGAGE Learning, 2012).

2. Lisa McCann & Laurie Ann Pearlman, "Vicarious Traumatization: A Framework for Understanding the Psychological Effects of Working with Victims," *Journal of Traumatic Stress* 3, no. 1 (January 1990), 131-149.

3. Elizabeth Aparicio, Lynn Murphy Michalopoulos, & George Unick, "An Examination of the Psychometric Properties of the Vicarious Trauma Scale in a Sample of Licensed Social Workers," *Health & Social Work* 38, no. 4 (November 2013), 199-206.

4. "Economic and Social Bill of Rights," The King Center, Accessed August 31, 2018. http://thekingcenter.org/archive/document/economic-and-social-bill-rights.

FURTHER READING

Alexander, Michelle. *The New Jim Crow: Mass Incarceration in the Age of Colorblindness.* New York: The New Press, 2012.

Austen, Ben. High Risers: *Cabrini-Green and the Fate of American Public Housing.* New York: HarperCollins, 2018.

Baldwin, James. *The Fire Next Time.* New York: Vintage, 2013.

Borden, William. *Contemporary Psychodynamic Theory & Practice.* Oxford: Oxford University Press, 2008.

Brooks, Gwendolyn. *Blacks.* Chicago: Third World Press, 1994.

Coval, Kevin. *A People's History of Chicago.* Chicago: Haymarket Books, 2017.

Davoine, Françoise and Jean-Max Gaudilliére. *History Beyond Trauma.* New York: Other Press, 2004.

Desmond, Matthew. *Evicted: Poverty and Profit in the American City.* New York: Random House, 2016.

Duneier, Mitchell. *Slim's Table: Race, Respectability, and Masculinity.* Chicago: University of Chicago Press, 1992.

Ewing, Eve L. *Ghosts in the Schoolyard: Racism and School Closings on Chicago's South Side.* Chicago: University of Chicago Press, 2018.

Herman, Judith L. *Trauma and Recovery: The Aftermath of Violence—From Domestic Abuse to Political Terror.* New York: Basic Books, 1992.

Kotlowitz, Alex. *An American Summer.* New York: Nan A. Talese, 2019.

Kotlowitz, Alex. *There Are No Children Here: The Story of Two Boys Growing Up in the Other America.* New York: Anchor Books, 1991.

Lydersen, Kari. *Mayor 1%: Rahm Emanuel and the Rise of Chicago's 99%.* Chicago: Haymarket Books, 2013.

Mitchell, Stephen A. and Margaret J. *Black. Freud and Beyond: A History of Modern Psychoanalytic Thought.* New York: Basic Books, 2016.

Moore, Natalie Y. *The South Side: A Portrait of Chicago and American Segregation.* New York: St. Martin's Press, 2016.

Petty, Audrey. *High Rise Stories: Voices from Chicago Public Housing.* San Francisco: McSweeney's, 2013.

Rogers, Annie G. *The Unsayable: The Hidden Language of Trauma.* New York: Ballantine Books, 2008.

Scull, Andrew. *Madness in Civilization: A Cultural History of Insanity from the Bible to Freud, from the Madhouse to Modern Medicine.* Princeton, NJ: Princeton University Press, 2015.

Simon, David and Edward Burns. *The Corner: A Year in the Life of an Inner-City Neighborhood.* New York: Broadway Books, 1997.

Stevenson, Bryan. *Just Mercy: A Story of Justice and Redemption.* New York: Spiegel & Grau, 2014.

Taylor, Flint. *The Torture Machine: Racism and Police Violence in Chicago.* Chicago: Haymarket Books, 2019.

Wright, Richard. *Native Son.* New York: Harper Perennial, 2005.

RECOMMENDED ORGANIZATIONS

The following is a list of organizations working to reduce the disparities discussed in this book. Big issues require equally large imaginations, whether the focus is upon the healthcare disparities in the LGBTQ community, the lack of affordable mental health services, or the long-term ramifications of mass incarceration. Social work is nothing if not diverse, and each of the below groups manage to embody the values my profession holds dear. A few caveats: there are a plethora of nonprofits doing valuable work, and the following list is by no means meant to be comprehensive. Better to think of it as a list of fellow travelers I've encountered in my own journey. Also, this list is unavoidably Chicago-centric, but their work is worth noticing, and, if such needs are unmet in your community, perhaps this can serve as a roadmap to a possible solution.

Community Renewal Society
(www.communityrenewalsociety.org)

Community Renewal Society is a progressive interfaith coalition of faith leaders and congregations from a variety of traditions who do the on-the-ground work to organize the communities they serve. They primarily focus on issues related to employment, housing, education, criminal justice, and the many ways in which all of those areas intersect.

Groupe interdisciplinaire freudien de recherche et d'interventions cliniques (GIFRIC)
(www.gifric.com)

The psychoanalysts of GIFRIC have done much to bring to help practicing clinicians grasp the rewarding but complicated work of Jacques Lacan. For over thirty years they have run a 24-hour center for young adults with psychosis, the 388, which offers a whole range of services that has greatly reduced hospitalizations for their patients.

Howard Brown Health
(www.howardbrown.org)

Howard Brown is one of the largest LGBTQ organizations in the country. They offer both physical and mental health services as well a host of other programs that benefit the LGBTQ community. All of their care is provided in a warm, affirming environment that really puts their patients first. I often refer my LGBTQ patients to them so they can receive robust, affirming healthcare.

The International Society for Psychological and Social Approaches to Psychosis
(www.isps.org)

ISPS seeks to bring together both mental health professionals and persons with lived experience of psychosis in order to prioritize humane approaches to treatment that respect the dignity and worth of those with serious mental illness.

The Kedzie Center
(www.thekedziecenter.org)

Chicago has long had a frayed system of mental health providers for those with no or little insurance even before Rahm Emanuel slashed the number of publicly funded clinics. Some therapists had seen the writing on the wall years before and worked to fund clinics in a novel way: If local residents agreed to a small property tax increase (an average of $16 per household), they would be guaranteed services at a center in their community regardless of ability to pay. The Kedzie Center is the first such clinic in Chicago which would be noteworthy by itself, but they also focus on doing in-depth, psychodynamically-informed work with their patients as well as a variety of outreach events in the community.

The Night Ministry
(www.thenightministry.org)

If you drive around Chicago late at night you may see one of their buses in an area where people experiencing homelessness usually gather. Their buses offer basic healthcare services, condoms and necessary medications, case management, and a warm cup of coffee to those with few other options. They also recognize how profoundly lonely homelessness can be and work to develop connections with their clients.

Psychotherapy Action Network
(www.psian.org)

This relatively new organization was formed by my colleagues at the Chicago Center for Psychoanalysis just a few years ago. Like me, they are concerned about the prevalence of the disease-based model of mental illness and the increasing marginalization of long-term, person-focused therapy by overly rigid short-term models.

READI Program at Heartland Alliance
(www.heartlandalliance.org)

Heartland Alliance is a massive non-profit in Chicago that does great work around poverty and immigration, but I'm particularly excited about this relatively new program. Guided by Senior Director Eddie Bocanegra, himself a former gang member who shares his story in Alex Kotlowitz's An American Summer, the program seeks to reduce gun violence by connecting men most vulnerable to being a perpetrator and/or victim to jobs while offering them ample support along the way.

Smart Decarceration Project
(voices.uchicago.edu/smartdecar)

This project affiliated with my alma mater, the School of Social Service Administration at the University of Chicago, seeks to understand the many ramifications of mass incarceration and work to help individuals as they transition back to their communities. Recent projects have focused on deferred prosecution programs and helping probation officers better serve those with mental illness. Dr. Matthew Epperson, the project's director, spoke at my graduation and his words continue to inspire me to this day.

Young Chicago Authors
(www.youngchicagoauthors.org)

The alumni of this organization form the backbone of Chicago's vibrant music and poetry scenes: Chance the Rapper, Jamila Woods, Saba, Noname, Brittany Black Rose Kapri, Eve Ewing, Nate Marshall, and José Olivarez, among others. Young Chicago Authors works with young people to help them express themselves through poetry and hosts the annual Louder Than a Bomb Festival, the largest youth poetry slam in the country.